THE SACRED PATH WORKBOOK

Also by Jamie Sams

Midnight Song: Quest for the Vanished Ones

Medicine Cards™: The Discovery of Power Through
  the Ways of Animals (with David Carson)

Sacred Path Cards™: The Discovery of Self Through
  Native Teachings

Other Council Fires Were Here Before Ours
  (with Twylah Nitsch)

The
Sacred Path
Workbook

NEW TEACHINGS AND
TOOLS TO ILLUMINATE
YOUR PERSONAL JOURNEY

JAMIE SAMS

HarperSanFrancisco
A Division of HarperCollins*Publishers*

Illustrations by Linda Childers

THE SACRED PATH WORKBOOK: *New Teachings and Tools to Illuminate Your Personal Journey.* © 1991 by Jamie Sams. Printed in the United States of America. No part of this book may be used or reproduced in any manner whatsoever without written permission except in the case of brief quotations embodied in critical articles and reviews. For information address HarperCollins Publishers, 10 East 53rd Street, New York, NY 10022.

FIRST EDITION

Library of Congress Cataloging-in-Publication Data

Sams, Jamie, 1951–
   The sacred path workbook: new teachings and tools to
   illuminate your personal journey / Jamie Sams. —1st ed.
     p. cm.
   ISBN 0–06–250794–X (pbk.)
   1. Fortune-telling by cards.   2. Self-realization—Miscellanea.
   3. Indians of North America—Religion and mythology—Miscellanea.
   I. Title.
   BF1878.S27 1991
   133.3'242—dc20   90–56440
                                                              CIP

91   92   93   94   95   RRD(H) 10 9 8 7 6 5 4 3 2 1

To Brooke Medicine Eagle and Barbara Marx Hubbard
for their work for the Children of Earth,
which is done in the name of love.

Contents

The Cards

Acknowledgments

My heartfelt thanks to the following people for bringing my dream into the hands of so many others: Clayton Pathfinder, Tom Vision Maker, Barbara Dreamweaver, Robin Sun Swan, Ani Walks With Beauty, George Soaring Eagle, and Barbara Skyarcher. Being of the Harper Tribe, you each have helped me, and I say to you, "Nya:weh Skennio," thank you for being.

Author's Note

As we each strive to grow and change in new directions, we are reminded of the lesson of the many spokes on the Wheel of Life. Each of us will stand on every spoke of the Medicine Wheel. At some time or other we will all walk on similar trails through the forest. The time for hierarchy is over; every man, woman, and child on this planet is a Medicine Person. It makes no difference who or what we are, what training we have had, or what race we come from. If we would all use our healing abilities to heal the inner conflicts in our lives, we would have the right to use that Medicine to assist others. All humans have been given the mission of healing themselves. The inner peace of self-healing can restore our Sacred Space and that of All Our Relations. In accomplishing this common goal we will bring world peace into reality.

I believe that we can all be Medicine Persons in our own right as long as we each tend to our own personal healing. Medicine Persons are not necessarily Native American, Tribal Aborigine, or Mongolian Shamans, rather, we are all responsible for working very hard on ourselves and sharing our discoveries of our personal healing paths with others.

I know that I am learning the same lessons on a daily basis that I am writing about. I grow and change; I fall on my face; I laugh and I cry because I see no fault in being human. I get angry with myself, I become determined, I find creative solutions to the questions I pose to myself, and then I move forward again. This workbook is as much a gift to me as it is to each of my Sisters and Brothers who will find it helpful.

The long and arduous journey we all agreed to take on this Earth Walk is difficult, but it can be filled with joy. It is my intent to use my abilities to assist the Planetary Family as we all grow together. I am opinionated when it comes to inequality. I know that it has created worlds of separation that have been the barriers to our common spiritual evolution. The use of the Medicine Cards™ and the Sacred Path Cards™ seems to be a great equalizer. The cards do not distinguish between the high and mighty and the meek. We can choose to see our challenges or to deny the messages presented because we have free will. Great Mystery has assured us the equal opportunities we need in order to make those choices. However, if we choose to deny or not remove those barriers that keep us from evolving, we will stagnate and die as a human race. Using this workbook will allow you to see your progress.

I believe that truth is found in every path, and so I honor all traditions, races, and creeds. The tools that come from all walks of life are valid sources of personal progress. If the teachings of the Red Race have touched your heart, I am grateful—this was my wish in creating all of the cards. I am very happy and thankful for the loving support of all those who have written and expressed their growth and change.

I am trusting in my personal process and the common goal that leads each of us through the fires of our own fears. I find that the pain of moving through my illusions is always replaced by the exquisite joy of internal and eternal peace when I have the courage to face my self-created limitations that have gripped me in a stranglehold. I trust that each of you will find the assistance you need to grow and flourish as you find faith in your true Selves and your connection to the Great Mystery. The Sacred Path is the Pathway of Beauty, and we are walking it as *one*. If perchance our paths should cross, it will be good to look into your eyes.

Jamie Midnight Song

The Purpose of
Using a Workbook

A workbook enables any seeker of clarity to record progress made during the time period it is used. In our modern world, it becomes easy to forget the winning situations that allowed us to make stable gains in our lives. Once a problem is solved or a challenge met and conquered, we are off again on to other things. The agony of the fearful moment is forgotten as trivial when we see the bright light of a new morning. We often forget, in our joyous victory, to be grateful for the tools that allowed us to get through the darkness.

If we use a journal to record our victories or a workbook to mark the steps along our Sacred Path, we are then more able to note the patterns of our lives and to see how we set goals, meet challenges, create solutions, and better ourselves. Unwanted habit patterns or chronic situations that limit our personal growth can be readily changed once we discover them and choose behavior alternatives that will enhance our lives.

This workbook is a tool that gives further understanding of the lessons we all must learn on the Sacred Path of human experience. I am sharing new information in this text in order to assist readers in becoming self-reliant on their individual Pathways of Beauty. The Sacred Path Cards™ are merely mirrors to allow every person to reflect upon the inner knowing that is Great Mystery's gift to all of humankind. In using this card system, you are developing skills to assist you in the processes of intuition, gratitude, wisdom, Earth connection, manifestation of goals, compassion, and a multitude of other abilities. While these skills are learned and sharpened, the process can be recorded as a reminder that we each have the ability to meet any challenge presented on the Good Red Road of physical life.

This workbook can be a confidant, a counselor, a teacher, a diary, a memo, a progress report, or a self-improvement manual. Its purpose and uses are up to you. However you choose to use it, the workbook can catalog the manner in which you have chosen to structure the your growth process. When we learn to use old information in a new way, many fresh ideas arise and the creative process begins once more. With this workbook, we trust that the new skills presented will allow you new opportunities for growth.

The *Sacred Path Workbook* can be used on a daily basis, a weekly basis, or whenever the desire or need arises. It is designed to serve your needs. If you are confused or desire clarity in a situation, the workbook should offer certain solutions for specific problems. I looked within and saw many of the prominent challenges presented to our human family through the eyes of others who have asked for assistance. I have chosen several ways of assisting the questioning human mind and heart with the new card spreads presented here. The interpretation of each spread and how it applies to your situation is up to you. If practiced, this applicable skill portion of using your intuition will help you to develop a new sense of inner knowing.

Empowerment is really self-mastery. This is not to say that you need to conquer life, but rather that you learn and master the talents and abilities that allow life to be an experience in joy and balance. These human living skills are reflected back to us through the Creature-beings of the animal kingdom. The more we learn about how our planetary counterparts have mastered physical life, the easier it will be for us to follow those leaders and live naturally again. Each new lesson can be learned best through the living of it. Unless the teaching is put into practice, the seeds of wisdom fall on fallow ground. Progressively recording the lessons we have learned and how the new understanding applies to our lives will bring the accumulated wisdom full circle.

Sometimes, when we have learned a skill we can automatically create new ideas with the utmost simplicity. The attention or energy that would be spent on carefully learning the new skill is no longer necessary. That extra energy can then be used to create further uses for the ability. The more any talent is perfected, the easier it is to use. As each of us develops our living and inner knowing skills, we are allowing more energy to flow through us. This is called particle flow by scientists. The faster the energy flows, the less we are resisting our divine right to wholeness. The more we hesitate or limit ourselves, the slower the energy flows. The more we learn about ourselves, the less we resist the future and the unknown.

The Pathway of Beauty is based on balance and our willingness to walk the Earth in a balanced manner. Many of the unhappy Two-leggeds in our Human Tribe do not enjoy the lessons of physical life because they feel that they do not possess the talents or potential to meet the challenges placed in their paths. Their resistance to being in physical bodies and walking the Earth Mother during this exciting time of change stems from their fears that they cannot find happiness on our planet. Of all of the Earth Tribes we, Two-leggeds, have been given the mission to learn through being limitless knowing spirits who chose the limitation of physical bodies in order to feel and touch the lessons of the heart. This workbook is one of the many tools along the way that will allow the discovery of being human to be a joy-filled one. The tools that teach us the Sacred Path come from All Our Relations, but the empowerment of using those tools is self-created—and that is Good Medicine!

How to Use This Workbook
by Sections

The Sacred Path Workbook is set up in sections that will allow each reader to examine the various aspects of the Sacred Path Cards™ that reflect the Traditional Teachings of the Red Nation. You will also learn how those lessons may be applied to modern life-styles.

NOTE: Always look at the actual cards used in every example so that you can relate to the medicine of each one.

Section One

In the first section, we will examine the cards one by one. Each card has a lesson that all humans can learn and master during their Earth Walks. There are challenges to fully developing any skill in life. These challenges can be met easily if you know what detours or hazards have been placed in the road. Therefore, I have listed the challenges I have discovered as I came across each lesson in my growth process. You may find other challenges that I have not included that may apply to your personal situations. Once we recognize a challenge that has come our way, we are more able to meet and best that demanding task in order to be our personal best.

As we examine each card individually by picking a daily card or lesson we can then become aware of how we can meet and jump over each hurdle along our individual paths. The "Individual Applications" represented in each card allow us to look deeper into the modern application of these ancient Native American truths. In this way, we can see how we are creating our own individual Paths of Beauty, what challenges we might expect along the way, and how we can handle each task by clearing the resistance to growth before it becomes a problem.

Section Two

In section two we will examine some new spreads I have developed to answer specific questions that may arise from time to time. The text of this section is called "New Spreads." It explains how each card spread can assist you in accessing needed information that will further your understanding of a personal situation.

Section Three

Section three contains "How to Use the Cards to Contact the Ancestors in Spirit" as well as an application of practical usage of the cards called "Exercise to Contact the Spirit World." In this section we will look at a new spread called the "Red Road/Blue Road Spread," which I designed as a tool to show each of us how the Spirit World assists the Two-leggeds on the Good Red Road of physical life and to show how to access that knowledge.

Section Four

Section four explains how to use the Medicine Cards™ in a new way by adding one of the Blank Shields, as well as how to use the Sacred Path Cards™ along with the Totems of the Medicine Cards™ deck. "Using the Totems with the Sacred Path Cards™" will help us examine how to use both decks together, using specific examples and exercises so that you will become proficient in seeing the double messages presented.

Section Five

"Using Both Decks to Find Your Path of Beauty" will help to further enhance your understanding of how to use both decks to give deeper meaning. I have designed a new spread called the "Beauty Way Spread," which is introduced in this portion of the text. We will look at how to further the skill of using the Totems with the Sacred Path Cards™ and apply it to this new card spread. Then you will be given the opportunity to pull your own cards and determine how your individual cards can be interpreted with your new skills.

Section Six

Section six allows room for your personal journal of notes, which will record your progress. I have added a few questions that you may ask yourself while recording the results of your spreads in order to gain further understanding of your path. I have provided many pages of notes throughout the book and several pages of daily and weekly progress sheets at the end of the book.

SECTION ONE

How to Use the
Individual Applications

Along with the applications discussed in the *Sacred Path Cards™*
book, each of the forty-four Sacred Path Cards™ have further
applications that are covered in the following pages. This section
of the workbook allows you to seek deeper understanding of any
one of a card's lessons and to view the wisdom and the challenges
as an initiation step. With this understanding, you will be able to
work through the lesson in your own way depending upon how
the lessons apply to your circumstances.

In working on one aspect of your situation you can pull
one card and apply its singular lesson to your life. In so doing,
the lesson of that card may be learned and another solution may
appear. As always, you are free to discover which of the many
meanings, challenges, or lessons of each card apply to your situation. In using this portion of the workbook, seekers are given
many ways to apply the questions asked or challenges mentioned.

Every person's experience will be different. The cards are
designed to help you develop a sense of knowing rather than to
give flat answers. My purpose in designing section 1 in this manner was to offer abundant applications and food for thought. The
number of levels of experience that every person can reach in this
style of self-examination is limitless. Because we are each unique

and have different needs, it is most appropriate to allow each seeker to discover why and how the card's lesson is meant in as many different situations as possible. This is the Sacred Path of the Self discovering the Self.

Please note that each time you pick a card, its application may be different as you approach your growth process in new ways. There is a timelessness to truth that will expand your understanding with each new life experience. The key to personal illumination is trusting your process.

As you delve deeper into the creative ways you have chosen to experience life, you may see a pattern in the cards. You may come up with many of the same cards over and over again as you meet different aspects of each lesson. This pattern assures you that you are creating every type of situation in order to meet each lesson's challenges head on. This is not the time to pick at your shadow and say "I thought I had already learned that one!" in disgust. In trusting the process, we meet every aspect of our challenges and know the joy of completion at the end of the trail. You have created the repeat lessons to make you stronger and more self-assured, so now your task is to find opportunity in the growth pattern.

This section of further individual applications is intended to allow you to find the forgotten pieces of the puzzle and to construct your picture of life in wholeness. The reminder presented in every card that you pick is *the time is now and the power to find needed solutions lives inside of you.*

The Cards

1

Pipe

PRAYER/INNER PEACE

ATTRIBUTES
Giving praise for peace • Showing gratitude for blessings
• Feeling serenity/At-one-ment • Experiencing life with ease because of inner balance •
Balancing male and female

CHALLENGES
Resolving inner conflicts • Creating the solitude of a quiet mind • Lacking appreciation
• Silencing internal dialogue/chatter • Coming into alignment with All Our Relations •

The Cards

Individual Applications

The Pipe card teaches us the balance of male and female, outer world and inner world, as well as the truth or illusion that dwells in all things. When we are grateful for every thought and action in physical life, we may then appreciate the importance of those experiences as we further understand how these lessons have assisted our growth. There can be no inner peace unless we quiet the mind and reflect upon the here and now. The Pipe can assist us by stopping us long enough to *smoke* Our Relations by bringing the goodness of their Medicines into our lungs and bodies. In so doing we are, in effect, seeking union with the other Earth Tribes that represent our Planetary Family.

In choosing the Pipe card, we are put on notice that it is time to stop everything and seek inner peace. Perhaps the world is moving too fast or our dreams are slipping away because we have forgotten what is really important. In some instances, we may be forgetting to ask for assistance and consequently are being worn down by our own treadmill of daily activity.

The Pipe is reminding us that there is a world outside our troubles or woes that is waiting patiently for acknowledgment. The natural beauty of the outer world is merely a mirror view of what is living inside of our beings, hidden in safety, draped in the solitude of a silent mind.

Nothing can impinge on the peace that is *earned* through knowing and loving the Self. We love others, we love beauty, we love the world around us, and yet we often see ourselves as unimportant or unworthy. When this attitude is existing within our hearts, we may defend our *right to be* by putting on airs or misrepresenting who or what we are. To lie to another is a grave error, but to lie to the true Self is deadly. Much inner conflict may arise from the need to be right. The Ancestors and Allies of nature will continue to love us unconditionally as we move through our Earth Walks, but our true Selves will be riddled with inner conflict if we insist on holding on to the lies and illusions that keep the false sense of well-being in place.

The Pipe gives us one way to find the inner peace that will relieve the anguish of a heart torn by fear. Illusions that have created walls between the self and the true Self can be the one major barrier to inner peace. The Pipe allows us to send our gratitude and at-one-ment to the Great Mystery in order to come into alignment with our true Self. Although this is often a painful, gut-wrenching process, the outcome can be one of the most profound actions in our lives. When we take in the smoke of the Pipe, the spirits of All Our Relations can mingle with us and assist us in unveiling the truth of who or what we are. If we ask for assistance, the Medicines of every Relation are set into motion and the illusions of separation can be flushed out.

The Sacred Pipe Ceremony can be used as a symbol in our lives to serve as a reminder that inner peace is needed at this time. If we have found the inner peace we sought, we will see the Pipe card as a validation of the personal work we have completed. When inner peace is found, there is a kind of magic that occurs in the outer world whereby the Creature-beings no longer run from us but feel us as their true friends. The hurry of the modern world melts away and nothing seems to threaten our existence. The pettiness of others cannot affect our lives, and we are suddenly very happy to do nothing or everything with total joy.

The Pipe represents our prayers for assistance in finding this magical inner peace and our praise for the help received as we work toward that goal. The solitude of a quiet mind and content-ed heart is a rare quality in today's world. It begins with each of us and our willingness to rid our minds of illusions and separate-ness. Peace on Earth begins within and is the one way every human being can bring the Pipe of Peace to All Our Relations.

2

Sweat Lodge

PURIFICATION

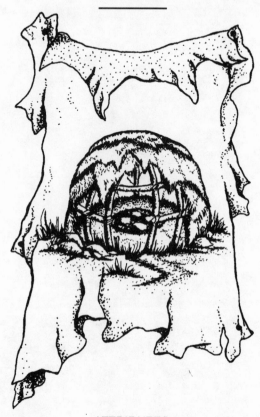

ATTRIBUTES
Dropping old habits or limitations • Clearing the mind's negativity
• Cleaning the Spirit's rust • Detoxifying the body •
Cleansing feelings that create separation

CHALLENGES
Becoming willing to let go • Entering the Earth Mother's womb with humility
• Acknowledging what needs to be purified • Using prayer to affect purification •
Moving energy • Following purification with new attitudes and actions

Individual Applications

In drawing the Sweat Lodge card, you may be asking for a cleansing. When we are hurt or stressed by life's initiations, we tend to ignore the signals that our minds and bodies are giving us. The stress habits that are masking our agitation or pain may be smoking or drinking too much, eating junk foods, sitting in boredom rather than exercising, gossiping, and so on. This mental and physical "rust" will keep us from being balanced. In preparing for any new venture or need for change, it is wise to purify the old. This purification can mean finding the courage to confront the habits that undermine our welfare, then calling on the Medicine that will assist us in removing the blockage to our path.

On the physical level, a short fast, a steam bath, or more exercise may be needed. The body is the vehicle of the spirit and allows us to express the gifts and abilities that Great Mystery gave us. Without proper balance of body, mind, and spirit, our lives can become strewn with mental, emotional, or toxic physical litter.

The Sweat Lodge is the symbol for purification and relays many messages. In drawing this card you are being put on notice that some area of your life is in need of change through purification before you can take the next step of your journey. Your ability to examine your life with a "cold eye" and not buy into your denial or justifications will help you see how this card applies to your present situation. You do not need to judge the things needing to be purified but rather look beyond them to the hurt, indecision, or frustration that caused them.

The road to self-examination is a rough one and should be accompanied by a contrite heart and humble attitude. Giving thanks and acknowledging the need for support is the beginning of purification. To have the courage to let go of the ego and ask for assistance is a virtue that many have lost in the modern world. The more often we seek the silence and commune with Great Mystery and those Ally Spirits who desire to assist us, the easier the path becomes because we are no longer alone.

The Sweat Lodge is made of willow, the wood of love. We can feel this love when we re-enter the womb of our Earth Mother, which the lodge represents. It is necessary to approach the purification process with gentleness and love, never being the "critical parent" by making little of forward movement (your own or another's), however small. The inner child needs to be nurtured as we purify, so that the hurts that *caused* the imbalance can be understood and released with compassion. In the Sweat Lodge, the Earth Mother's womb, we ask for loving blessings to come to those we do not understand so that unity may be accomplished. If you are confused, ask for assistance in finding clarity through purification so that the thing that needs to be released can be understood and achieved.

In drawing this card, you are being given the opportunity to purify or to deny the rust you have collected. You may find that the barrier to your progress is removable if you handle it one piece at a time with caring and deep conviction. The process of purification may not happen overnight if you need to change a lifelong habit, or it may occur as quickly and simply as a shift in your attitude. All in all, the Allies of the Sweat Lodge—the Willow, the Fire Spirits, the Water Spirits, the Pipe, the darkness of Mother Earth's womb, your gratitude, the Spirits of the Ancestors, the Relations or Allies of the prayer ties, the Stone People, and the Sacred Songs that honor Great Mystery—will assist you if you have the courage to ask and receive.

In all cases, the ultimate goal of purification is a new attitude followed by action. Whatever action it takes to purify the old toxic energy is appropriate to use at this time. You may need to employ compassion, forgiveness, will power, or any number of your talents. Love is the needed attitude and the needed action is your willingness to become the purified Self.

3

Vision Quest

SEEKING/FINDING

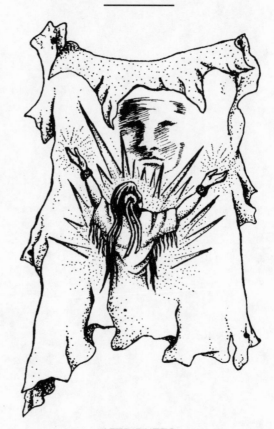

ATTRIBUTES
Looking for answers • Finding solutions • Asking and being willing to receive
• Envisioning the future • Discovering your purpose •

CHALLENGES
Surrendering or giving over to Great Mystery • Becoming willing to see truth
• Learning how to use solutions • Knowing that you are a part of the Divine Plan •
Asking for guidance •Using vision for a life map

Individual Applications

If you have chosen the Vision Quest card, you are being put on notice to open your eyes and really see. See what? The world around you, the ocean, the mountains, the life-force in every living thing. See that every thing and every person is your teacher. If you have been denying the potential you carry, see that. If you have been denying the beauty of life, see that. If you have been denying the precious gift of life, see that. In each instance, we are asked to seek solutions to what we are ignoring, denying, or refusing to acknowledge.

From the new viewpoint of awakening your senses, you may now feel free to look at other things below the surface of your perceptions. Is it time for you to rattle the cage of self-inflicted limitations and shake your life up a bit? Has boredom gotten the best of you? Are you ready for some excitement that could very well mean the birth of a new you? If so, look at what would give your heart the greatest joy in life. Acknowledge that desire as a goal that you can accomplish. Then begin your individual-at-home Vision Quest by asking Great Mystery for a signpost or road map to assist you in finding your way on the Sacred Path. This can be done anywhere, even in a city apartment. Just use your imagination in order to surrender to the free flow of the wind, anoint your body with the tides of the oceans, curl your toes in the Earth Mother's soil, and fire up your passion for living a life that supports you. Then be willing to receive the messages or visions that Great Mystery sends your way.

You may choose to do this little exercise, which is helpful in finding your way. Bathe your body and clean out any thoughts that would distract you before retiring to sleep. Eat nothing the next morning and take a walk in nature. Find a peaceful and untraveled location where you can sit and be still until you can *Enter the Silence* of a quiet mind. Open your heart and ask for some sign from nature as to which Creature-being, Stone Person, or Standing Person can assist you in your quest for new direction. Observe everything around you in silence and see who speaks to you. If a leaf falls, go to the Standing Person who called you through its leaf and listen. If a Dragonfly crosses your path, ask what it is telling you about illusions. If a Hawk circles overhead, listen for its message. If a Stone calls to you, ask what its Rock Medicine is. That night, sleep with an object you found in your specific area and allow your dreams to instruct you. You may eat the following morning. *Note: It is not necessary to fast while doing this process. The fasting portion of this exercise is not to be attempted by anyone with blood sugar or health problems.*

All avenues are open to those seeking a vision or a new direction who approach Great Mystery with a need, an open heart and mind, and a willingness to experience the love available from All Our Relations. If you have drawn this card, you are being asked to decide which area of your life needs clear vision. It may be that you need a new direction or a new conviction. Drawing this card may be a sign that change is coming but the change needs solidity or structure. The structure needed may be given to you in a dream, a vision, or a life-changing experience. Whatever the future holds for you is about to appear in some form. Tests of character and initiations are not needed to prove our worthiness to others. Initiations are experienced in order to allow us to discover our true Selves. Many personal talents, strengths, and gifts are rarely used by humans except in times of crisis. The Vision Quest card says that now is the time to find the potential of your true Self in order to understand your place in the Divine Plan.

In all instances, the Vision Quest card marks a time of seeking answers and gives the assurance that what is needed can and will be found. These visions, solutions, answers, or life maps may not appear as you expect them to, but you will be given an answer. The key is to observe everything and to make sense of the messages. The truth will feel right. You must actively seek and be willing to face truth with courage and joy in order to find it.

4

Peyote Ceremony

NEW ABILITIES

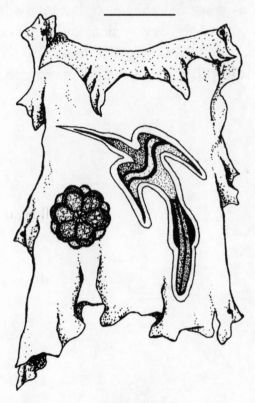

ATTRIBUTES

Reclaiming skills • Acknowledging the talents now emerging
• Employing new tools to conquer life's challenges • Embracing your potential •
Using the new gifts being offered

CHALLENGES

Using these new abilities with courage • Risking setbacks while learning new skills
• Letting go of old tools that did not work •
Discovering how new talents will best serve you • Developing the new talents fully
• Acknowledging the Self's right to use the abilities to take charge •

Individual Applications

In drawing the Peyote Ceremony card, you are being asked to transcend the fears, limitations, destructiveness, and imprisonment of some facet of your life. It is time to find a *new* path to the crack in the universe where you may reconnect with the raw creative force of Great Mystery. This is in no way to suggest that you are to take power substances. To do so without the reverence of ritual and prayer or the guidance of a Medicine Person is sheer foolishness. The opening that you are seeking is to be found in another way; through your own path there will be an opportunity presented.

The Peyote card is putting you on notice to become aware of the opportunities that will allow you to discover something new about yourself—to acknowledge the gifts you have not fully developed and to use those gifts as a magnet to pull the raw, creative energy from the crack in the universe to you. It may be time to discover the infinite possibilities that are presented in the now. If you have somehow felt that you are being imprisoned, look at the ideas that you have bought into that represent the ball and chain. It may be time to let go of stifling relationships that bind your creativity and limit the use of your talents. Anytime you are accepting limitation as a way of life, you are burrowing deeper into the quicksands of suffocation and self-imprisonment. If you have ever asked yourself, "Is this all there is to life?" you know what I mean. The key is in asking yourself how you can rediscover the skills you already have in order to create a new path.

Life will present you with the opportunities that you seek if you have the courage to face the chaos of your fears. Mescalito may be called on to assist you in this underworld journey without ingesting Peyote. The spirit of this Sacred Plant is a Guardian to the dimension door that leads to the crack in the universe. Our world contains polarity of experience: the light and shadow, the pleasure and pain, the boldness and shyness, the heights of courageous living and the depths of fearful cowering. All of these expressions of our humanness are the pathways to growth. The Peyote Ceremony card is imploring you to seek the opportunity in every situation so that you will no longer avoid or judge the lessons and experiences of life.

In acknowledging the potential beyond the crack in our personal universes or realms of experience, we can see that beyond limiting thoughts there is always a new cycle of truth awaiting us. Through that new cycle of rediscovered abilities, we may further develop our talents by using them to aid the planet. Seek the change that will add to your present understanding of life, acknowledge the steps that brought you to that new knowing, and be willing to experience all growth with joy. The freedom of seeing the whole of humanity without judgment is the first step to oneness. If all pathways can be honored as being equal, we may accomplish the Whirling Rainbow that allows all races, all people, to contribute their gifts in peace.

Look to the place where your heart has held judgment or limitation. Then begin to remove the blockages that stop you from living with the abilities that represent your true nature. The Peyote Ceremony card and the crack in the universe promise a world where all will live as one. Each will contribute their truth to the whole as expressions of the true Selves who mirror the facets of Great Mystery's Creation. In all the magnificence and glory of the Original Source, all life-forms have the mission of using their gifts to the fullest. This is the essence of the Sacred Path: to find, develop, and use the gifts of the heart. It is now time to trust that you matter and that you are needed to complete the Divine Plan. The Great Mystery lives in all things and the denial of any ability or talent makes the whole incomplete.

5

Standing People

ROOTS/GIVING

ATTRIBUTES
Nurturing the root of your ability to give to yourself • Finding the root of your strength
• Acknowledging the ability to go deeper into self-awareness •
Balancing receiving and giving • Taking what you need, then sharing with others

CHALLENGES
Becoming willing to give and receive equally • Taking care of your needs
• Being grounded and present • Standing tall and proud •
Assisting others, not rescuing them and making them helpless

The Cards

Individual Applications

If you have chosen the Standing People card it is time to reach to the roots of your being and search for some truth. In some way, you are in need of nurturing. If the opinions of others have masked your personal truth, it is time to seek the silence under a tree and ask to be reconnected with your Sacred Space and your Sacred Point of View. If you have caught the *busy* or *hurry* disease and feel disconnected from the Earth, *stop,* then go walk in natural surroundings until you feel rejuvenated. If you have been doing any journeying or out-of-body travel and you need to balance your body with your spirit in this world, then garden, walk, swim, or do any physical activity that will reconnect you by replacing the roots you inadvertently pulled out of the Earth Mother when your spirit went flying. In other words, find the root of the imbalance and correct it. Then you can give yourself another chance at the present situation.

The Standing People card may also ask you to look at the root of a difficult situation that you are now facing. The truth of any circumstance may be discovered through finding its root, which you can do by asking certain questions of the Self.

How and when did this situation actually begin?

What has been feeding the situation to bring it to its present status?

Have I been forcing it to grow with my expectations? Or have I been allowing the joy to be choked by the weeds of my fears?

Have I acknowledged the lessons created through my present path?

Is a lie or the opinion of another blinding me to the truth?

What personal truth or understanding could assist me in turning this situation into a joy-filled one?

Am I willing to give or receive nurturing through reconnecting to my roots—the center of my Sacred Space?

In all cases, the Standing People teach us the lessons of giving and receiving unconditionally. If you are controlling others or allowing others to control you, you are not Walking in Balance. If you are taking without giving gratitude, your thoughtlessness is being noticed. If you are afraid to give to others or if you give with strings attached, you may be forgetting your roots, which are deep in the Earth Mother. Mother Earth makes no demands on you for the gifts of food, shelter, the air you breathe, or the love she shares freely and abundantly, but it is up to you to take in what you need. When you are fed you may then share with others from your fullness.

Do not give too much without allowing others to return the flow. This form of caretaking or rescuing may stifle someone who could learn to be self-reliant if given the chance. The recipients of your giving also have root systems and need to use them. The basis of this situation is usually the caretaker's refusal to give to or nurture the Self, therefore it becomes necessary to give too much to others. The receivers of your attention will resent the smothering, and your friendship could explode.

To refuse to take in what you need through your own roots is foolish; to give until nothing is left for you to survive on is folly. To refuse to share with others or give of yourself will set you on a lonely trail. The selfishness found in some humans is a result of their not knowing how to give to the Self, perhaps because they weren't cared for by others in times of need. The Standing People teach us how to balance all of these lessons in giving and receiving, and then to stand tall and proud.

Remember that Willow is the tree of love because it is willing to bend with the wind, touch the Earth Mother, and reach for the stars. We use the Willow to make the frames of our Medicine Shields because love always bends and grows full circle, giving and receiving in kind.

6

Sun Dance

SELF-SACRIFICE

ATTRIBUTES
Sacrificing barriers • Ridding the Self of limits • Dropping hesitation
• Sacrificing personal fears • Going beyond suffering into joy •

CHALLENGES
Finding courage • Confronting limitations • Challenging the personal best
• Letting go of shadows • Connecting to the Tree of Life •

Individual Applications

If you have chosen the Sun Dance card, it may be time to reach out and ask if your talents can serve the Children of Earth. Possibly there is some aspect of your life that is in need of change, but that will take great courage to alter. If you make that change a symbol of your own personal Sun Dance, the courage you need may come to you. This shift may take longer than the four days that it takes to Sun Dance, but it will be far more gentle as well.

If you have been unaware of the role that women have taken to promote the growth of future generations, or if you have scorned the pain they endure during menstruation or childbirth, perhaps it is time to look at those attitudes. Women suffer through labor but find joy when the child is birthed.

Since sacrifice originally meant "to make sacred," this may be the time to begin seeing the sacredness of every act of life. In ridding yourself of limitation, hesitation, or refusal to take right action, you make your life sacred. To restore that inner knowing, you may wish to examine how you see each act you perform in physical life. In seeing every action as a learning situation, you may then find the way in which that act serves your growth. In using every movement to its fullest, the beauty of your willingness to learn from each action will feed your life with joy.

The Sun Dance card provides many lessons on the courage you will need in order to sacrifice those parts of your life that limit your capacity for happiness. You must look and see which lesson applies to your life. The Sun Dance card's reminders are that you have the courage to see your own vision, that you are a sacred part of the Tree of Life, and that all life needs your Good Medicine. If it is time to admit to yourself the blunders that have hurt you or others, you may need to sacrifice guilt or blame and begin again with love. To dance in the light of Grandfather Sun and show yourself and others that you are willing to change and grow is the gift you give yourself through learning the lessons of this card.

The keynote of self-sacrifice is the willingness to sacrifice the parts of the unhealed self that are not performing in a sacred manner—the shadowy parts of our natures that keep us from enduring until we come to completion. We are not asked to deny our needs. We are not pushed to refuse our heart's desire but, rather, to eliminate the thoughts or actions that keep us from true happiness. The balance found in supporting the true Self is in our willingness to persevere in the dance of life. The action called for is to clear our least desirable traits. The endurance of spirit that is willing to leave no stone unturned is the strength of the Sun Dancer.

In preparing the Self to endure the rigors of self-sacrifice we must make our bodies strong. Our minds must be free of negativity and our emotions must be freely expressed. Our limitations must be set aside and a willingness to be supported by the Great Mystery must be in place. This preparation is the Eagle Bone Whistle's call to the spirit of the true Self. The cry of Eagle marks the point at which we are willing to sacrifice our tunnel vision and fly. We have made our lives sacred when we make our actions of self-sacrifice stand for who we are, where we are going, how we intend to get there, why we choose our path, and how we intend to change. The Sun Dance reflects these lessons of Grandfather Sun's light in our lives and teaches us what to sacrifice and when.

In all cases, the Sun Dance card represents the act of making all things sacred. We begin by eliminating those aspects of Self that cling to limitation; then we can dance the dance of Creation. We end the dance of this Earth Walk by sacrificing the bodies that gave us a way to dance. We are born again into the Spirit World where our sacrifice is in preparing for our return, to dance in the physical world again and reconnect with the Tree of Life. Each cycle of beauty teaches us the sacredness of every spoke on the Medicine Wheel of Life.

7

Medicine Wheel

CYCLES/MOVEMENT

ATTRIBUTES

Signaling the end of stagnation • Noticing that the doors are now open
• Finding new direction • Noticing the green light—go now •

CHALLENGES

Confronting the fear of movement or the next step • Answering the wake-up call
• Observing proper growth cycles and using them •
Benefiting from movement • Being willing to change gears and grow

Individual Applications

If you have chosen the Medicine Wheel card you are being asked to notice your personal growth in a way that will allow the changes in your life to become more meaningful. Nothing is outside of the Wheel of Life that the Sacred Hoop represents. If you are at a loss as to which path to take, look at the four colors of the Four Directions. Which of the four colors immediately comes to mind? Look to the next few paragraphs for help in deciding which direction can be a guide for you in your present situation.

In learning to use the Medicine Wheel as a divining rod to find your next step in personal growth, look at the attributes of each direction.

Yellow—Forward Movement Through Illuminating New Ideas

In the East is Illumination and the determinism of male energy. Eagle lives in the East and has a better overall view of life, balanced with the freedom of spirit that soars through the sky closest to the light of Grandfather Sun. The Golden Door is in the East and can take you to new ideas and new levels of awareness and aid you in conquering your greatest spiritual challenges.

Illumination will always come to those who are willing to look at and remove their self-imposed hesitations or limitations. Eagle is the symbol of the freedom of thought and flight that assists those willing to take the chance and seek new horizons. This is the message that you may need to remove the fear of change. Or it may be time to listen to new ideas and take a chance by trusting your male demonstrative side. Journey to the Golden Door and beyond with Eagle. Only then will you know the joy and freedom of your newfound understanding.

Red—The Child Within Becomes Your Teacher

In the South, we find a need to reconnect with the faith, trust, innocence, and humility of the little child. If this is the color that came to your mind, you are being urged by the child within you to stop that adult jazz and chill out! The irreverence of this tricky little kid is begging you to laugh away your seriousness and see the ridiculous way you are behaving. If you have lost faith and/or trust, pick up those rose-colored glasses, shattered as they may be, and for your own good stick them back on your out-of-joint nose. If the inner child is hurt, comfort that part of yourself from the adult-self's nurturing viewpoint. Then do something you always wanted to do as a child but were forbidden to do. That ought to instill humility in the serious adult-self and give you a few laughs. The innocence will return if you allow that inner child to talk to you and teach you.

Black—The Bear Tells You to Be Quiet, Listen to Your Heart, and Feel

The Bear is here to aid you in knowing that you hold all the answers inside yourself. You have a female side that is receptive. It's time to use it now. In connecting with this color, you have asked to Enter the Silence of a still heart and mind to find your own answers. This is the "looking within" place on the Medicine Wheel. The opinions of others do not apply in this step of personal growth. Remember that in seeking the truth of your own heart, the feelings of the female side of your nature are valid. To feel is to heal. If you cannot feel what is true for you, it may be like Grandpa Shongo told Grandmother Twylah when she was small,

"If you are in the West at the 'looking within' place, be sure that your bottom isn't sticking out when you are looking within. The Bear may bite it off." That is why the place of Introspection is the place of Entering the Silence. To enter is to be all the way inside your Sacred Space in silence, willing to listen and receive.

White—The Buffalo of Abundance Brings New Wisdom and Asks for Gratitude

In the North, the place of the Elders, we find the wisdom of many winters. Each cycle of life's changes is marked by experience that gives us the wisdom of insight. When in doubt, go to one who has walked a similar path and seek the counsel of the white-haired ones who walked the Good Red Road before you. These Elders feel sad because they have the wisdom of experience and want to share it, in order to assist others in avoiding the hazards of movement. But many youngsters are too busy and impatient to honor the gift the Elders represent. Abundance is created by using the gifts of life to the fullest, receiving these gifts in gratitude, and thereby creating space for more abundance to flow in. This is the wisdom of the North. Ask yourself if there is something you are not using or taking advantage of, then give it away or use it. Seek the Old Ones who know how to use the gifts you have been given and listen to their counsel. Find out if you have forgotten to acknowledge someone for a job well done, and praise them in gratitude for their contribution to all of Earth's Children. This will remove the blockages you may be feeling about not being appreciated yourself. Then you may share the wisdom you have gained with others who seek similar answers.

In all cases drawing the Medicine Wheel card is the signal that big changes are coming. The cycles of your life may take a very different shape if you are willing to feel the joy the changes bring and to drop your fear of them. All beings are asking themselves questions so that they may come to the place of knowing within their hearts. The heart of the Sacred Hoop is the Whirling Rainbow that contains all colors, all experience, all paths, every pleasure of life, and every point of growth toward wholeness. You are being called to notice each color and hue, each tone and placement of the Whirling Rainbow you are creating in your personal circle. Then it will be time to welcome the changes that will allow all creatures to join together as one.

All in all, drawing the Medicine Wheel card is telling each of us to honor the lessons we grow from. See the value of the present changes from a new perspective and remember that nothing ever stays the same. We travel the Sacred Hoop many times in our Earth Walk. With each circle we travel, a new sense of Self and others is achieved. To keep these perspectives in balance we must always remember that we will stand on each spoke of the Wheel and walk in another's moccasins. There is no room for judgment when these Knowing Systems of wisdom live in our Sacred Space.

Your Notes

8

East Shield

ILLUMINATION/CLARITY

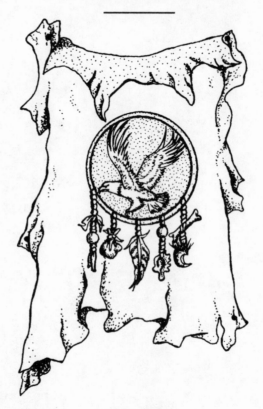

ATTRIBUTES

Understanding life in a new and focused way • Knowing now replaces old beliefs
• Expanding your point of view • Embracing the male energy of the Seeker •
Gaining spiritual understanding, enlightenment, and freedom

CHALLENGES

Facing inner doubts • Removing confusion or disbelief • Seeing the whole picture
• Limiting your ability to know •
Fearing freedom of thought or expanded awareness

Individual Applications

The East Shield card holds many lessons for those seeking to be their own person. When the light goes on in your head and you suddenly know the truth, you have come to the understanding of the East Shield. Personal knowing is the keynote in picking this card. If you are seeking what is right and proper for your present path, you are seeking spiritual illumination. To know when you have found that illumination is to feel the heart's joy. If your heart is happy and you are full of new ideas and ready to implement them, you have reached that Golden Door.

Eagle may be pecking on your chest with its beak trying to open your heart to the wonders of new understanding. This Sacred Medicine Bird knows the spirit trails of the Sky Nation and may be the Ally that teaches you to fly. Journeying out of body with Eagle can give you a way to release any disbelief that may limit your capacity to see and know.

If you chose the East Shield card, it may be time for you to look at all three paths to Illumination and see if one needs some clarity or clearing. Are you ignoring your talents and creativity and therefore allowing limitation to haunt the trail of personal expansion or true freedom? Do you need to recognize a trait that keeps you from focusing on taking flight? Is the poison of confusion feeding self-doubt? Or have you been in a rut for so long that you do not believe there are any other sunlit trails through the Sky Nation?

These and many other lessons may apply if you look deeply at the lessons of the East Shield. The lessons may come in the form of knowing how and when to share your thoughts, your joys, and your pain, or in knowing how to look at your value system. How much value do you put in your material possessions, your health, your ideas, your Sacred Space? Is balance needed to remedy a lack of confidence? If you are too caught up in the material world, give away those things that weigh you down so that you will not crash before you feel the freedom of flight.

The East Shield also speaks of shedding the old skin of worn out habits and identities in order to clearly see once more. The ideas that represent personal focus, clarity, and vision are carried in Eagle's talons. The power to transmute the poisons that keep you from the freedom of flight are the property of Snake. The national symbol of the Mexican flag is the Eagle eating the Snake. Eagle ate Snake to ingest Snake's Good Medicine. It was then that Eagle could protect the home of lofty ideals, for Eagle had learned to transmute the poison that would destroy freedom of thought. After all, Illumination *is* freedom and clarity of thought.

The gentle reminder of the East Shield is that all things have energy. Energy is always being exchanged; the foods you eat, the air you breath, the goods you acquire, the money you use are all exchanging energy with you. It is always proper and timely to ask questions and seek clear answers as to your relationships with all that you contact and use in your life. From your answers, you will feel the clarity of spiritual understanding emerge, opening the Golden Door of Illumination in your life.

In all cases, Eagle and the East Shield implore us to be our personal best by seeing clearly the overall picture of our Earth Walk. Our destiny and our mission are always the same from person to person. We are to use the gifts we have been given to the fullest, walk in balance, seek beauty and harmony, and contribute our best to the whole. In order for these requirements to be filled, we must clearly see where freedom's light lives within us and hold that illuminating lamp high so we can see how to follow the Path of Beauty. Once we are clear about who we are and where we are going, our lives become an illuminating example to others.

9

South Shield

INNOCENCE/INNER CHILD

ATTRIBUTES
Embracing humility and trust • Having faith and childlike wonder
• Protecting and nurturing children • Becoming willing to be natural •
Playful physical activity • Healing childhood hurts

CHALLENGES
Facing arrogance • Feeling too old to start again or learn
• Refusing to believe in magic • Believing in trust and love again •
Healing the adult-self's self-importance and fear
• Breaking the patterns of family dysfunction •

Individual Applications

If you have chosen the South Shield card, it may be time to drop the masks of what others want you to be and focus on who you are and what you want to become. If the pressures of family, business associates, or friends have put you in a role that does not suit you, the path is clear. You must call upon the courage of the child within and risk taking a chance. Changing back to vulnerability and childlike trust is often scary to the adult-self but is very necessary in the discovery of wholeness. The patterns of family dysfunction are broken through healing the inner child and refusing to pass pain to the next generation.

You may have been sitting in the world of seriousness too long if the South Shield has appeared today. Life is for living. The joy of being in a physical body on our beautiful Earth Mother can evade you if you are creating a feeling of black clouds hanging over your head. Why not remember how to dance in the rain? It may be time to go to a park or playground and swing or go on the merry-go-round or visit a carnival. The most important part of the lesson is to laugh at yourself. Try a water fight with friends; the cleansing humor of the Water Spirits may make you feel young again. Whatever you decide to do, do it with joy and sensitivity. Remember that your inner child does not need to be hurtful or cruel. Children only use those tactics on their friends after learning them by observing their adult role models.

It may be time for you to start some exercise with others. If you do not play games or participate with others in a joyous way, life can become drudgery and will not bring the body into balance. If you enjoy running or swimming alone, do it. But some people find that these activities begin to feel like work. These people should find fun group activities instead. Allow your body to express its sense of grace and freedom in its own way. Allow the tension you have been holding to melt into the fluidity of movement that releases the old and brings a new sense of Self into play.

If you feel complete on these three lessons of the South Shield, it may be time to look at whether you have ever felt abandoned. Have you ever felt like you needed to cry but couldn't? Have you ever felt that you were stripped of part of your childhood? If your answer is yes, it is time to do those things for yourself that will heal your old wounds. The little child within you can be nurtured by your adult-self. This is an exercise in compassion that can heal the way you treat yourself as an adult. Do you think hurtful or abusive thoughts about yourself? If you said those thoughts to others would they be hurt? The time to care for yourself is at hand. Don't abandon yourself just because someone else did long ago. Don't fail to trust your feelings just because someone told you that you were wrong once. Remember that you can successfully find the wonder of life again if you give yourself time to correct your attitude and recapture the joy.

In being in the moment, you can see all three pathways to the South Shield and rediscover the child that loves you and offers to be your teacher. Your inner child may be zany, irreverent, precocious, and a trickster, but these exact lessons will take you a long way toward restoring the faith that you had as a child. You deserve to experience the pleasures of being childlike and natural. The refusal to allow your heart to grow old or cold is the first step in retrieving your innocence, trusting your process, and keeping the magic alive. In this manner you can open yourself to the same unconditional love that children naturally give.

In all cases, the South Shield teaches us to become humble as we drop our disbelief and cynical ways. The wonder of life is always alive in those who replace their fears with trust, reclaiming the magic of the child. The heart is healed in this manner and love can live again.

10

West Shield

INTROSPECTION/GOALS

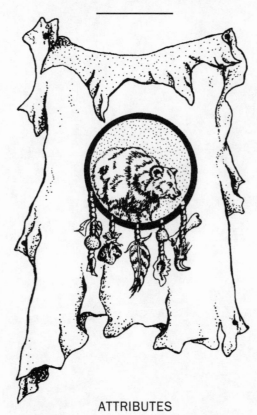

ATTRIBUTES

Finding your own answers • Going within to listen
• Taking care of tomorrow by making goals today • Being receptive to female energy •
Trusting that Great Mystery protects and plans the future

CHALLENGES

Fearing that you cannot know • Being afraid to receive or feel
• Fearing the future • Learning to trust your own answers •
Refusing to quiet the mind • No focus on goals/not having plans
• Owning and confronting the hidden thoughts or feelings that destroy the feminine •

Individual Applications

If you have chosen the West Shield card it may be a time to retreat from the hustle-bustle of rigorous activity or strenuous schedules. In using your male Warrior side to get ahead, you may have gotten ahead of yourself and thrown your female inner knowing into a spin. Strength comes from intuitive knowing (female) and walking your truth (male). If you have not taken the time to get in touch with the small, still voice within lately, do it now.

If your goals are unclear, follow Bear to the cave of silence and rest your weary bones for an hour or so. Then you may want to write down all of the things you have ever wanted to achieve in your present Earth Walk. Slowly digest these ideas over the next few days and cross off those you have completed or that no longer apply. When you have finished, you may then seek assistance on how to reach your remaining aims by calling on your Allies or on a special Ancestor who has assisted you in the past. Be willing to receive the assistance of Great Mystery and honor the wisdom sent your way.

If you have had some difficulty in the past with finding your personal truth, the West Shield may be showing you a different approach. Stop listening to the opinions of others and listen to your heart. Does it make you happy to hear from others why your ideals are too difficult, if not impossible, to obtain? Do you hear a different drummer and dance a different step? If so, follow those joyful movements and sounds, and let yourself receive the inner knowing that comes from being in sync with yourself.

Nobody else walks in your moccasins. If they are trying to, it will just give both of you corns or bunions.

On the other hand, the West Shield may be calling to you for a different reason. Female-receptive energy is not only the willingness to go within, but also the willingness *to feel* the sensations that allow our knowing to be experienced on a physical level. This gift has been called "women's intuition." We all have it; in men it is sometimes called "gut feeling." The West Shield is where it begins. To honor our perceptions and impressions, we must avoid the deadly mistake of not paying attention. When we feel something, it is time to be introspective and see if that feeling has validity. It is far too easy in this modern world to ignore our own warning systems and then say later, "Oh my, I did feel something was amiss, but I put it out of my mind." Remember, the mind is not where we feel—that is male reasoning.

The West Shield's reminder is that each of us needs to develop the ability to receive answers, abundance, love, joy, awareness, knowing, and nurturing. This must be balanced with the Warrior-nature of the East Shield that allows us to put those gifts to use in a constructive and forthright manner. The digested ideas of the West Shield give us the structure for reaching our goals and nourishing them along the way. The answers live inside of us, and we may give them birth and a voice anytime we are ready to Enter the Silence or enter the cave of Bear.

In all cases, the Bear calls you to take a brief hibernation in order to sense your inner truths. How you use these answers and precious thoughts to meet the future and give it birth in the now, is a personal lesson. Each being is unique and holds a special piece to the universal puzzle. All seekers are solely responsible for the pieces to their personal puzzles. Where the two worlds meet (the inner world of feeling and the outer world of physical reality), we find the cave of Bear. Being in the world and not of it may not work anymore if we are willing to tackle the future and ensure life on the Earth Mother. Bear's dream for humanity is that each Two-legged will find the inner answers of the West Shield that can heal the Self and, in turn, be at one with the Self and in harmony with All Our Relations.

11

North Shield

WISDOM/GRATITUDE

ATTRIBUTES

True knowing or wisdom based on experience
• Acknowledging the opportunity of every lesson learned •
Having earned knowledge through learning all the steps to the lesson
• Giving thanks for all lessons no matter how difficult • Praising for all lessons •
Connecting to the Elder within the Self

CHALLENGES

Using wisdom properly • Returning thanks to the Source
• Refusing to claim knowledge not earned • Honoring wisdom in others •
Honoring wisdom in Self • Walking your talk

Individual Applications

If you chose the North Shield you are being asked to look at all three paths to wisdom and gratitude. Listen to the Earth Mother, the omens, the signs and portents. Listen to the Creature-beings and trust their guidance. Listen to others who have different ideas and customs. Expand your understanding of our world and your fellow inhabitants. Greet them with an open mind and an understanding heart, and through shared experience, wisdom will naturally follow.

In looking to the lessons of the North Shield, we find a need to honor the natural wisdom we carry, for as Native American Tradition states, we carry the wisdom of our Ancestors in our bones. We smoke the spirits of All Our Relations and become one with them. We observe nature and realize that all has perfect order that applies to daily living. This gift of wisdom comes through the experience of observation and cannot be learned by reading about it. We earn this wisdom by taking time to reflect on everything we experience.

In embracing these ideas, you may care to ask yourself if you have been denying what your heart knows as truth. Have you acknowledged the inner knowing or intuition that you carry? Has some situation brought the words of wisdom or advice to your lips when you least expected them? If so, it is time to be grateful for the wellspring of knowledge, common sense, and understanding you have available. On the other hand, it may be time to learn that unasked-for advice or information is not welcomed by others who are seeking their own inner source for answers. This inner source is where the Great Mystery lives within us.

It may be time to seek truth and justice in your daily life. Don't let pride stand in the way of understanding and peaceful living. Allow others their truth even if it differs from yours. There is no need to change your Sacred Point of View or to get your feathers ruffled because others don't agree with you. Know that you are solely responsible for your actions and for your inner peace. Be grateful for this and all blessings. Remember that free will is the blessing that has allowed all of us to experience life in order to learn the lessons that lead to wisdom. It is often more difficult to be grateful for the uncomfortable lessons; they also allow us to grow no matter how much we resist them at the time they occur.

The North Shield has many trails that eventually lead to the Council of Elders. Seek the counsel of those who have walked the road before you and honor the experience they have gathered. The Elders of every race and nation seek to share what they have learned so that they may pass on their truths. Many fear dying without being able to give the gifts of knowledge they hold. A part of the wisdom of youth is to know the value of the Elders and to joyfully acknowledge the living treasures that they represent. You may be in time to share those treasures if you are reminded by this card to take responsibility for the Medicine of wisdom that an Elder can pass on to you. Show gratitude to the teachers as a way of honoring the gifts they have given.

The North Shield is the symbol of all the lessons of the other directions on the Medicine Wheel that have been digested and applied. The wisdom needed at this time may be one of recalling the lessons you have learned and applying them to the now. The inner knowing that you carry is available when you are clear about your desired outcome. If you have not decided to act for the greatest good for all concerned, the Elder who lives within you may not impart the wisdom you need.

In all cases, the North Shield beckons you to grow, to expand, to know, and to use truth as the only guideline. It may be time to listen, time to share what you have learned, time to honor the advice of an Elder, or time to forgive. Find which applications of wisdom are needed for your further growth and allow the gratitude for the learning of it to fill your heart with the peace of knowing *how* to "Walk Your Talk."

12

Arrow

TRUTH AS PROTECTION

ATTRIBUTES
Walking your truth • Honoring your integrity • Seeing truth in all things
• Using your truth in a good way • Not needing to defend who you are or what you know •
• Honoring the ideals of brotherhood or sisterhood •

CHALLENGES
Fearing that you do not know your own truth
• Giving advice you don't follow yourself • Fearing to speak your truth •
Owning your mistakes by not always having to be right • Refusing to be honest
• Allowing others their truth • Protecting yourself by compromising your integrity •

Individual Applications

If you have chosen the Arrow card you are being asked to review the people in your life that you feel connected to in a loyal and committed way. Look at the beauty of each of them and notice what type of example they set as role models for you. This is the beginning of developing the sense of family that will support your Warrior nature. In looking at the beauty of others and being willing to receive the lessons they impart just by being who and what they are, there is no longer any need for jealousy or envy.

Another message of the Arrow card is that no matter how great the struggle of any challenge, your Warrior nature has the strength to meet and conquer the obstacles. When you feel as if your last ounce of energy is gone, you can call upon the Medicine of a Brother or Sister who has bested a similar situation by using truth, and in so doing, feel their strength and integrity enter your heart to aid you.

If Arrow is bringing a time of self-examination, you may wish to ask yourself some of the following, challenging questions, which point to using truth as your protection. Have I aimed straight and true in my opinions, decisions, or goals? Do I sense a lack of Brotherhood or Sisterhood in my life presently? Has competition stopped me from seeing the value of others, and is it therefore stifling my natural desire to make true bonds of friendship? Am I being honest with myself and others in my present situation? Do I have the courage to stop criticizing others? Can I honor the paths that others choose without insisting that my way is better? Has my self-importance made me believe that I cannot learn from others in a loving and constructive way?

Arrow may be asking you to do something that will call for bravery on your part. Completing that task might allow you to walk your truth and find a new side of your Warrior spirit. The satisfaction of knowing that you did something that you might have not believed was possible before can bring forth the best of your gifts. It may be time to acknowledge those gifts so that they may be used again in the future.

Arrow may also be calling you to put yourself out in the world by following the truth of the Warrior within. This chance could be entering a new career, becoming a single parent, opening your own business, sharing your hidden feelings with others, using your healing abilities, or doing any of a multitude of other things. The truth you hold is the reflection of your heart's greatest joy. When you follow the heart, you follow truth. When you ignore the truth your heart naturally carries, you are setting a trap for yourself. The Self can lose sight of the original target when the joy of the heart's truth is not present, making the Arrow fall short of the goal every time.

Arrow warns us not to take on the projections of others when their confusion is present. Arrow teaches us to be connected to the heart of the Warrior-self who is willing to take action in bringing the truth to light. This Warrior-self is always courageous and willing to face all truths, even when they hurt. The Warrior within sees how and why the truth can heal.

In all cases, Arrow is calling upon your deepest well of inner strength and courage so that faith in your growth process can be restored by the truth that lives within you, unhindered by deceptions. When you feel as if the world is presenting you with conflicts that are too heavy to carry, Arrow is your reminder to aim higher—to seek and find the hidden side of your Warrior nature and then use it to honor the truth inside your heart.

13

Coral

NURTURING

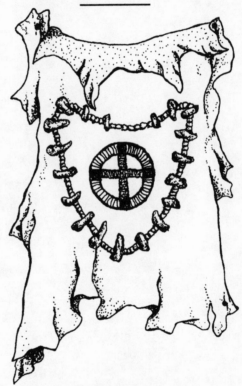

ATTRIBUTES

Giving to Self • Accepting love • Being loving and compassionate
• Assisting the growth in others • Being fed by the Earth Mother •
Honoring the feelings of others • Feeding your needs

CHALLENGES

Knowing how to properly nurture • Stopping abuse of any kind
• Healing past betrayals • Breaking patterns of family dysfunction •
Receiving nurturance • Showing compassion for the Self
• Not expecting others to fill your emptiness •

Individual Applications

If the Coral card has shown up in your spread today, it may be necessary to review how you nurture yourself or others. You may want to ask yourself if you understand what your personal needs are. These are not to be confused with goals. Needs are very specific. Nurturing comes in the form of meeting your needs rather than catering to your superficial compulsions. Your body is a good place to begin. How much sleep does your body need? Does your body react to foods that are too rich, sour, sweet, acidic, or spicy? Do you ignore these warnings? Can you dance your body's expression? Will you allow yourself to sigh if you feel emotion welling up inside you?

Look at how certain situations make you feel. Do your feelings run high when you force yourself to go to business oriented parties? Does your body feel stressed when you refuse to exercise it? Is your day so full that quiet times alone have become a thing of the past? Have you forgotten to laugh at yourself and allow the child within you to play? Do you want to scream sometimes and let the body release its tension but swallow your frustration instead? Are you so busy doing things for others that your needs have been ignored? If your answer to any of these questions is yes, your sense of personal needs has been upset in some way.

Coral says to listen to your body; find what nurtures you and do it! To walk gently and in balance is an art. We must each learn what is necessary for our personal enhancement and well-being. In so doing, we may then begin to see how the other creatures of the Planetary Family are examples of this nurturing. Coral is the reminder that we all carry red blood and all are Children of Earth. Our needs may be different from those of others, but every creature has needs. In relying on others to supply the nurturing that we must supply for ourselves, we can follow the crooked trail. To achieve balance we may learn to connect with our Earth Mother and receive our nurturing from Her as well as through our own actions. When we are adept at nurturing ourselves, then we have a base from which we may share with others. When each being is a whole person they no longer look to others expecting to be fulfilled. In this manner each whole person may share totally and completely without fear of losing something or of being used by another in the process.

Coral is also a reminder that the Ancestors and their gifts live through your blood and in you. If you are feeling weak or vulnerable, call on those who walked the Earth before you and be willing to ask to share their Medicine and their strength. In this way you are making an effort to heal patterns of dysfunction or abuse and to create compassionate, loving environments, which will nurture the growth of all concerned.

In all instances, the Coral card points to the idea of nurturing in its *action* form—not thinking about it or wishing for it but *acting* on it. Giving nurturance to another without smothering the recipient is a part of this lesson. Nurture the dreams you carry by working with the energy of the dream daily. Nurture the child within by clearing old pain and giving that child freedom of expression. Nurture the body through dance, exercise, good foods, or sexual intimacy. Nurture your abilities by working on the skills that make them better. Nurture your relationships with others through being thoughtful or caring. Nurture your connection to Great Mystery and the Medicine Helpers through prayer. Nurture your career connections through communication. Nurture your emotions by clearing the feelings that were too painful to accept at the time. Nurture the Self by strengthening the body, heart, mind, and spirit. Nurture the future by helping children. All of these aspects of nurturing are ways to insure continued growth. Our ability to respond to the nurturing we need in our lives depends upon our ability to use what we know and how we feel in order to grow.

14

Kokopelli

FERTILITY

ATTRIBUTES

Productive/Inventive •Tapping your creativity • Readying for enrichment
• Bringing ideas forth into being • Making way for abundance •
Maximizing your potential • Fertilizing your field of dreams
• Using available energy for growth •

CHALLENGES

Preparing for growth • Acting in a timely and proper manner • Being impatient
• Thinking infertile thoughts • Trusting your own creations •

Individual Applications

If Kokopelli has enchanted you with the magical flute and its mystical music, you are being asked to nurture the magic inside yourself. Get rid of your skepticism and learn to trust your heart. Follow the song of your inner flute that plays a tune only your heart can hear. It may take courage to tear yourself away from the rational excuses that haunt your true desire in order to create fertility in your life, but there is no time like the present. Go for it!

The Kokopelli card marks a time of spontaneity and abundant creation. Everything you touch will bear fruit if you act on your own sense of inner timing. You may hit every green light in town without having to brake once. This sparkling synchronicity is no accident. You are in balance and trusting that internal magic. The seeds you plant now will bear fruit if you trust your green thumb and nurture the growing dream.

Kokopelli is also a reminder of the fertile ground available for new projects or ideas. If you were waiting for the proper time to bring up that needed raise or to approach a peer with an idea for a project, now is the time. Any major change you would care to make in your life will be fruitful as long as you are doing it because you want to rather than because it is expected by others. If you are doing anything for the wrong reason—anything that will not maximize your potential—the intention will fall on fallow ground. The fertility you could then expect would be the creative inventiveness you would need to get yourself out of the mess you created by going against your own wishes in order to please another.

The magical flute of Kokopelli called The People to trade with him. If you need new material fertility to support your chosen path, it may be time to trade in your car, or trade your outlook for a new one, share your dreams with a friend, barter something, trade goods that you no longer need, or find a new activity that will bear fruit. Trading one type of fertility for another is a good way to apply the lesson of Kokopelli.

On another level, Kokopelli can bring such abundance and fertility that there would be room for a Papoose in your life. If the Kokopelli card comes up with the Rabbit card from the Medicine Cards™ deck, you are assured of pregnancy. If it is not your desire to produce offspring at this time, you had better take extra precautions for a while. If, however, you and your mate have been planning to buy a Cradleboard, get it quickly; the Stork is about to deliver.

In all cases, Kokopelli calls us with the music of fertile magic. This mystical tune is full of the longing to be fulfilled. Every living being on Earth seeks fulfillment through actions, thoughts, and desires. If we want our dreams to manifest we must actively seek that fertility through our openness to all possibilities. Kokopelli cautions you to never limit the magic of life by closing your heart or mind. Fertile situations cannot enter the life of a person who cannot trust his or her personal creations and who destroys the potential for harvest through infertile thoughts or impatience.

The productive, inventive, abundantly creative side of our natures are the parts of our humanness that bring ideas forth into being. The keynote of the Kokopelli card is that all of these abilities are now available for proper and timely use. The moment is right; all elements are in place for taking the quantum leap into fertile creation. The only action that is needed is the human will-ingness to become the magic and do it.

We are humbly reminded that we are creative spirits made in the image of the Great Mystery and our mission is to respond to Creation.

15

Talking Stick

VIEWPOINTS/OPTIONS

ATTRIBUTES

Opening to new ideas • Giving yourself options • Expanding your viewpoint
• Listening to others • Being true to your Sacred Point of View •

CHALLENGES

Seeing alternatives • Avoiding tunnel vision • Being interested, not interesting
• Giving the Self opportunities • Allowing others an opinion • Trusting your truth •
Being willing to change if new facts are presented in truth

Individual Applications

If you have picked the Talking Stick card, you are being asked to listen to the thoughts, ideas, and input of others before speaking. Notice when others can broaden your viewpoint by sharing their ideas. The keynotes of the lessons afforded by the Talking Stick are based upon the following questions of self-examination.

Do I feel that I have to defend my Point of View?

If the answer is yes, observe which people, places, or things seem threatening to you. Then ask yourself why these things bring up your defense mechanisms. Does change in location threaten your Point of View? If so, remember that you have a right to express yourself wherever you are. Recall the times that you gave your authority to someone who was supposedly more knowledgeable or in a position of authority. Release that memory through breathing in deeply, holding the breath briefly, and then exhaling. Then immediately imagine yourself and your Sacred Space surrounded by the Whirling Rainbow of Peace.

Am I too busy to listen to others when they have something valid to say?

If the answer is yes, look at your ideas of self-importance and see yourself as one part of the whole of Great Mystery. Seek humility. If you do not seek humility, life will do it for you. You will create your greatest fears through lack of discipline. The discipline needed is accepting the present moment as an optional way of learning.

Have I forgotten to hear the whispers on the Wind and acknowledge my fellow creatures as they seek to enlighten me?

If the answer is yes, go to your favorite natural setting and reconnect with the Earth Mother and her children. Remove the disease of hurry from your life for a moment, Enter the Silence, and seek the wisdom of a quiet mind. Learn again the art of listening. Ask for signs to be given and watch all life-forms as they commune with you. Remember that life follows nature and the greatest lessons are learned through observation followed by experience. The new viewpoints in nature may surprise you.

The more alternatives we find through listening to the ideas of others, the easier our decision-making processes will be. Tunnel vision is deadly. When we refuse to try something new or see another trail through the forest we are robbing the Self of potential growth. The Talking Stick clearly points to every direction on the Medicine Wheel as being good and worthy of experiencing.

The Talking Stick also teaches us how to use communication skills from the Native American viewpoint, which is to share feelings, wisdom, teachings, customs, and Traditions without seeing others as wrong because they hold different Points of View. Native American understanding comes with the knowing that others will reveal their true natures and intent if we listen and observe. We know that our breath is sacred and our words come from our breath, therefore they are sacred. We will be remembered by our words and our actions. If we are not prepared to live the words we speak, we are dishonoring the gifts and talents that make up our power.

In pulling this card, we are being asked to review the aspects of our lives that deal with harmony through communication, exchange of ideas, and our personal methods of relating to others. Because we already know what we wish to impart to others, we can often learn more by listening to others than by talking ourselves. In seeing different ideas, we may discover new trails that offer opportunities for further growth.

16

Power Place

EARTH-CONNECTION/EMPOWERMENT

ATTRIBUTES

Feeling the joy of having a physical body • Owning the Sacredness of physicality
• Acknowledging health • Finding the Power Place inside the body •
Honoring the body's role and its needs • Feeling connected to the Earth Mother

CHALLENGES

Keeping physically fit • Bringing your spiritual nature into every physical act
• Staying grounded to Earth • Honoring your Earth Walk •
Seeing physicality as being equal to spirituality • Learning to love being human
• Using the gifts of body, mind, and spirit in unity and balance •

Individual Applications

If the Power Place card has come into your spread today, you are being asked to reconnect with the Earth Mother and share your celebration of physicality. When we find a Power Place in our outer world we are asked to also acknowledge the Power Place inside of our bodies. For each person it may be different, but this place is where we each feel total connection to the physical realm of our bodies.

The Power Place card is saying, "Remember that being a part of your world's answer is having all of your talents available for filling the needs of the here and now." Be in the present moment and see it as a gift of life. When we reconnect to a location on the Earth Mother, we come fully into present time, and then we know that our empowerment is the power of loving, totally and unconditionally, everything that we are at every moment in our lives. This can manifest as loving our bodies, our health, our sexuality, our feelings, our thoughts, our ability to move with rhythm, our roles in society, or our blessings in life.

When we seek empowerment we need a tool to physically carry out our plans and dreams. This tool is the body. The needs of our bodies are based in Earth Connection, for they are made of the same elements the Mother Earth contains. Our bodies atrophy if they are overworked or not exercised or given freedom of expression. To ignore how we are connected to the Earth is to ignore the role our bodies play in our quest for wholeness. Health is the greatest gift we have.

To express our unique missions during our Earth Walk, it is necessary to connect to the Earth and our physicality. The sacredness of physicality has been destroyed by most religions on the planet today. To find the guiltless joy of being physical and using body, mind, heart, and spirit in balance is a rare ability. This is the true essence of Earth Connection and empowerment. The outer Power Place is a mirror reflection of the inner world where each of us comes to a place of awareness that speaks of the sacredness of our present forms being extensions of our true Mother, the Earth. There is no guilt in her making love with the Thunder Beings. She is fertile in order to feed all of her children. She moves and expresses her sensuality and her wisdom in equal roles. We are being asked to honor this same reflection of spirituality and physicality in ourselves.

Grace, pleasure, worthiness, health, sexuality, sensuality, wisdom, feelings, unconditional love, creativity, guiltless freedom of expression, and sense of wholeness are the gifts she freely gives to those who would seek shelter in her arms. The empowerment is in acknowledging these gifts of beauty in ourselves when we return to the Power Places that call us to them. These Power Places are mirrors of the inner beauty we each hold in our physical forms and of how that beauty is manifesting outwardly each time we free ourselves enough to express it.

The safety of the Earth Mother allows us to express that which we might not otherwise be able to bring forth. The expression of who we are is often stifled by old belief systems that hinder our personal empowerment.

The Power Place is a location that is totally safe for the individual. In this area we are able to confront our fears, be ourselves, express our feelings, review our innermost thoughts, and be the dream we are in a physical way. Once we reconnect to the Power Place, we may find it has always lived within us.

Your Notes

17

Moon Lodge

RETREAT

ATTRIBUTES
Taking a time of rest, reflection, and inner work
• Finding strength in nonaction and relaxation •
Honoring the need to take a break and regroup • Examining dreams and feelings
• Acknowledging the value of time-out •

CHALLENGES
Fearing being alone • Having to be still and feel • Taking time for the Self
• Seeing strength in nonaction • Stopping the World •

Individual Applications

Since the Moon Lodge card signals a time of retreat, you may feel a yearning for a much needed break. Whether you are male or female, the Moon Lodge is saying that you need to examine your feelings at this time and see how Grandmother Moon is weaving the tides of your emotions and dreams. If there is confusion, inner conflict, or turmoil, it is a sure sign that relief from a too-busy schedule is needed.

Female energy is receptive energy. If you cannot nurture yourself by honoring your personal needs, your female side is languishing. Everybody needs the nurturing a mother can give. Our formative years are greatly influenced by our mothers. If you are in need of mothering in your life, go to your true mother, our Earth. Lie on her soil and feel her life-force course through your weary or disconnected body. Swim in her waters, run in her sands, listen to her heart and allow it to reconnect with yours. There are no orphans on our planet; each Two-legged is a child of our Earth Mother. Examine how you feel when you leave the hustle-bustle of your everyday life and seek the love and replenishing energy of the Mother we all share.

The Moon Lodge card is a signal that some aspect of how you relate to women, to your female side, to your own body and its functions and cycles, needs examination. Feelings are the key to this understanding. How do you really feel about the role of woman? Is there a mistrust of women caused by some old betrayal? Do you have some healing that needs to take place from some indignity you allowed into your life? Was this indignity a result of lack of respect for Self, your body, men, or women? In your need to be nurtured, have you accepted or given love to a person that did not respect the sacredness of your intention? Have you honored and respected the sexual coupling you have experienced in this Earth Walk? These are a few of the questions that may bring up feelings that need to be released in order to clear your female side whether you are a man or a woman.

Blame, shame, bitterness, or remorse are barriers to accepting the pleasure and abundance of our Earth Mother's nurturing. In honoring those feelings and allowing them to be washed away by Grandmother Moon's tides, each of us can make room for the healing energy of our Earth Mother. Every Child of Earth is an extension of the bounty of Creation that represents future. To create beauty in the future we must release the past, take time to nourish ourselves in the present, and trust that the future will take care of itself because we are living in the moment. When the present is balanced, the black Void of the future is no longer frightening. Fear results when we do not allow ourselves to receive the strength, courage, sustenance, and nurturing of Great Mystery. The willingness to receive comes from our female side and comes into balance when we retreat from the world's activities and pause for reflection and rest.

A time of rest can give us the opportunity to increase self-awareness. We are given the chance to make goals, receive visions, rest an overactive mind, examine feelings, clear limitations, or do nothing for a change.

The Moon Lodge card always signals a time of finding a splendor that is rarely available in the modern world. This rare gift to the Self is actualized by stopping all worldly activity and taking the time you need to recollect your thoughts, feelings, visions, and dreams of the future. In all cases, the Moon Lodge card calls for a retreat in some way. It is now time be alone. Reflect on what this means to you personally. Remember, retreat does not mean desertion. In this context, retreat means taking the time to support yourself by regrouping your energies so you may find the strength to carry on.

18

Whirling Rainbow

UNITY/WHOLENESS ACHIEVED

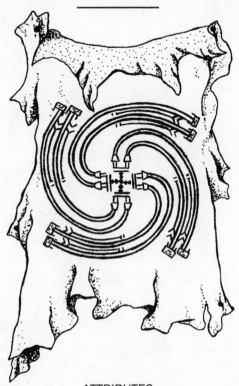

ATTRIBUTES

Honoring the wholeness of life • Acknowledging alignment
• Sensing no inner or outer struggle • Completing a goal or project •
Feeling at-one-ment with all life and at home with Self • Finishing a step or lesson

CHALLENGES

Recognizing healing • Acknowledging completion
• Judging accomplishments as not being enough • Refusing to take on other's issues •
Looking for everything that is wrong with the Self
• Unconditional love for the Self and others •

Individual Applications

If the Whirling Rainbow has entered your dreams, it is a sign that you are awakening to your potential. The wobble created by this type of healing may be occurring in your life and you may be confronting the parts of yourself that no longer apply to your present path. The disharmony of your old identity may still be in your Sacred Space; if so, it should be encircled with the Rainbow of Peace and allowed to dissipate on its own.

If you are asking for a peaceful solution in some area of your life, call upon the Whirling Rainbow. Ask the Whirling Rainbow to enter the dreams of any disharmonious person or unhappy situation in order to awaken those concerned to your peaceful intent. This action will bring you a new sense of harmony and inner peace. You are reminded that if others cannot see your desire to be a peacemaker, it is not your duty to take on their issues.

On another level, the Whirling Rainbow may be calling you to look at the unity or lack of it in your present situation. Is your purpose clear? Are you united in heart and mind? Do your words match your actions? If your focus has wavered, look at any opinions, judgments, or lies you may be carrying regarding the path you are presently on. Do these blockages match the feelings in your heart? If not, toss them into the Whirling Rainbow to be washed clean by the life-giving rains. There is no use in allowing doubts to be magnified in your Sacred Space. These types of blockages only serve to confuse and eliminate progress. Doubts create disharmony and judgment of Self and others.

Unity is the key word to the Whirling Rainbow card. Remember that Warriors of the Rainbow are the women and men who look inside their Sacred Space to do battle with those parts of the Self that destroy harmony, as opposed to soldiers who look outside to fight the parts of themselves they see in others. Maintaining unity may mean leaving the arena where others insist on fighting you and each other. We are not walking the Earth Mother to create the illness of diversity and separation.

Warriors of the Rainbow are the forerunners of the Fifth World of Peace, and peace begins with our sense of wholeness. Wholeness is achieved when we have removed the wreckage of separateness that blocks our ability to find unity with the Self. This type of healing allows us to supersede the unrest that may be present in the world around us. If we make time to acknowledge the moments when we feel that we have completed some lesson, healing process, or goal, we can achieve wholeness or closure in that area. Then we can move to our next lesson without feeling like we have lost an opportunity to enjoy the fruits of our labors. Taking time to feel the thrill of our new states of awareness brings unity with them. Wholeness will then be easier to recognize in the future. Completion should always be celebrated.

Life presents opportunities for us to achieve unity and wholeness at every turn if we are willing to acknowledge every tiny step along the way. It may be necessary to release the idea that our accomplishments are never enough. If you are still hurting from a lack of appreciation or acknowledgment, it is time to begin doing this for yourself.

In all instances, the Whirling Rainbow speaks to us of the way in which we view the interaction of our bodies, hearts, minds, and spirits. If these parts of the Self are in harmony, we have begun the process of working in unity. As we release the struggle or resistance in each aspect of our lives, we make room for new levels of awareness to appear. These new ideas are freed from our subconscious when we acknowledge that our last lesson is complete. When we move forward and grow further into wholeness we are asked to love each opportunity and to celebrate each success. The whole person then finds her or his connections to All Our Relations full of new unity because unconditional love and inner serenity mark their sense of wholeness.

19

Painted Face

SELF-EXPRESSION

ATTRIBUTES
Showing true Self • Acknowledging true abilities • Being your personal best
• Expressing talents without self-importance • Sharing skills and aiding the whole •

CHALLENGES
Confronting your vanity and ego • Fearing judgment of your expression
• Refusing to use creativity • Lacking self-worth or confidence •
Fearing losing face or failure

Individual Applications

Painted Face insists that we own our talents as a part of our total expression of Self. In this manner we are walking in balance and beauty without feeling the need to puff up the ego. To stop the flow of creativity is to cut the tie to the Creative Source, Great Mystery. Feelings are to be trusted so that Self-expression may flow. The rewards of expression are the gifts of experience and wisdom that every life-form brings to the Council Fire of Creation that sparks the light of the world.

In examining the way in which we express ourselves we must look at the inhibitions that may block the Path of Beauty. Vanity or self-importance can stop the flow of the true Self's natural way of being. The truth is that behind vanity's mask is an inner beauty that has been covered and buried. Riddled with fear, this inner beauty may have felt that it was not as real as the physical beauty that houses it. Genuineness of character needs to be allowed to come forward to make vanity drop its mask.

The fear of expressing who and what we are is often based in a fear of being different or unacceptable. These old ideas are tied to wanting to belong and to be admired by others. The ropes that tie us to the opinions of others can be cut if we are willing to stop our own judgments about how things should be, how people should act, what others should wear, and what is sensible.

You can begin by cutting the ropes of limitation and examining your belief systems that were formed when you were young. It might be advantageous to list the items that were *should not's* and *never do that's* in your experience. Then see which of those unspoken rules are limiting your self-expression. After seeing the limiting effect of the old ideas, you may choose to write new decisions about those *don'ts* and make a list of positive ways to express yourself without the old guilts or fears. The silly list of old negatives may include such items as wearing stripes with prints or writing with your left hand. Some other entries could reflect rules about kissing on a first date or singing in public. As you make the list, you will naturally go deeper into your serious issues and you may cut the cord to your fear of Self-expression. Painted Face reminds us that there is no failure in those who have the courage to express themselves. The only failure is in refusing to take the chance.

The Painted Face calls each of us to express our talents in a way that will assist the whole of Creation. In receiving this card, you are being asked to list your assets in order to express them through art. The artistic and creative side of this exercise is to decide which gifts could be expressed through a particular color and/or design. You are unique and so are the gifts you have to share with humankind. Paint your face and look at the reflection in a mirror. Then decide when, how, and with whom you wish to share your gifts.

Painted Face can also be a reminder of broken promises. Have you told someone you would assist them by using your expertise and then refused or forgotten to do so? If this is the case, look at why you did not complete the offer. Were you afraid to use a talent that you were not sure of? Did you see that you were offering help that had not been asked for? Do not allow guilt to cause you to *lose face*. Remedy the situation by calling the person and telling him or her your true intention. Express your truth and then continue with your life.

Knowing when to express our views, our talents, our sense of self, and our love of being who we are is the last part of this lesson. The development of our self-expression balanced with appropriate timing is a lesson of discernment. Knowing when and how to share who we are depends upon our ability to face the challenges of this card.

20

Counting Coup

VICTORY

ATTRIBUTES

Mission Accomplished • Rewards have been earned • Congratulating a job well done
• Acknowledging achievement • Winning in life • Celebration in order •

CHALLENGES

Fearing success or recognition • Doubting that victory is real • Minimizing the victory
• Receiving rewards earned • Boasting versus graciousness •

Individual Applications

The Counting Coup card heralds a time of some sort of personal victory that will enhance life and assist the whole of humankind and All Our Relations. If this is true in your case, take pride in your accomplishment and let others speak of it rather than boasting about it yourself. You know what it is that brought joyous victory to your personal Medicine Wheel and so does Great Mystery. It has been felt as a Coup by the whole of Creation whether you know it or not. If you need further recognition or approval, it may be time to examine why. If you want to share a victory with friends, you may chose to give a Celebration of Life Feast or party. In this way, you are learning the value of celebrating and sharing your joy with others.

In some cases, the Coup that is being counted when this card appears may not be readily apparent. If you have been waiting on another person to make a decision that will influence your life, perhaps that person has done so, and now you are being put on notice that good news is coming your way. If this message applies, check out any unfinished business and be ready for happy or rewarding results.

In choosing the Counting Coup card, possibly you are being asked to define how you feel when you win in life. Do you take time to acknowledge yourself in a meaningful way? Are you happy when others achieve personal victories? Are you challenged by receiving recognition or success? Are you envious of another's accomplishments? Is it time to redefine your goals and use active means to accomplish them or have you ignored your achievements by rushing too many new goals?

If your personal victories have been few, you may need to examine your verbal commitments. Have you promised to do something that you have not done? If so, do it now or advise the person you made the promise to that you will not be able to follow through and get that person's acknowledgment. It can be a personal victory to confront those things that you said you would do but can't. In this way, the person expecting the promise to be fulfilled will no longer wait for you to do it. Then your focus may be directed to other areas of your life. Eating a little humble pie is actually easier than killing yourself by trying to fulfill a commitment that was hastily spoken. In so doing, you free your intention and can move forward once again.

By examining our words and waiting before we speak, we are recognizing the human tendency to offer assistance to those we care for without weighing the actions or deeds needed to fulfill the promise. In receiving this card, you are being asked to look at all words that are spoken in haste: words of anger, love, gossip, and pride. Each set of words can reflect a need for a victory over imbalance. If this applies to your situation, slow down and weigh the effect your words create. What would happen if those words were backed by actions every time? What would you and others experience? The wisdom of few words and a lot of positive action may be needed in changing this type of personal limitation. Positive action is a victory in itself.

The Counting Coup card always marks a time of adding integrity to your sense of Self through personal or shared victory of some kind. In all instances, a celebration of the Children of Earth's continuing growth toward peace is proper. Focus on the victories rather than the losses and praise the forward movement. Every race, every creed, every Tradition, or individual that wages battle on hunger, poverty, greed, control, hatred, separation, war, or ignorance should be remembered and celebrated. You may not know the names of the Sisters and Brothers that battle for harmony through inner growth but your hearts are one. The victory of pulling this card is that we are the victory when we dance in balance, live our words, and walk gently on the Earth Mother.

21

Rites of Passage

CHANGE

ATTRIBUTES

Moving in a different direction • Discovering that new paths are available
• Adjusting your sense of reality or attitude •
Earning the right to enter a new level of life • Growing/evolving

CHALLENGES

Succumbing to stagnation • Refusing to change • Denying the completion of last lessons
• Fearing the unknown • Becoming complacent •

Individual Applications

If you have chosen the Rites of Passage card, some change you are undergoing needs celebration or acknowledgment. The fact that change is occurring means that your path is not stagnate, rather you are experiencing a new growth process. This growth process can include adjustments in your reality or your attitude that ask you to stretch beyond your last zone of comfort. When the present moment feels like a pair of comfortable old moccasins, you may be reluctant to trade in that comfort for the growth that may give your identity a few blisters during the learning process.

The Rites of Passage card may also be calling us to acknowledge any completions or new beginnings in our present life cycle. Any type of completion signals that a change is around the bend. If we are finished with a lesson, it is timely to move on. One challenge to change, in this case, can be our willingness to admit that we feel complete and therefore the prior lesson has ended. The change of completion has occurred whether we acknowledge it or not. The next change we can expect is the appearance of a new lesson.

Rites of Passage can also challenge our unwillingness to pass through our present lessons to get to a new cycle. This unwillingness is always supported by fear, doubt, and lack of trust. If this applies to you, it may be helpful to focus on the beauty of the new trail rather than on the steps necessary to get there. See for yourself how this could apply to your situation and drop the negatives—the can'ts, don'ts, and won'ts. When a positive attitude is maintained, it will be easier to take the final steps of the present lesson because the change needed has occurred. In this case, the change was a change in attitude.

In some cases, the Rites of Passage card is saying that you are now in transit, moving into another level of learning, which may be physical, emotional, spiritual, or intellectual. If this is your situation, greet this new state of being with joy and embrace the present transition. Every transition point in our lives marks a Rite of Passage, which is a test we give ourselves in order to conquer the barriers. We mark each passage by remembering the lessons.

Remember that there is no death without rebirth. If someone you know is graduating into the Blue Road of Spirit, assist their safe and speedy release by allowing them to go without your emotional needs blocking their path. This is the final Rite of Passage in any individual Earth Walk. Every Two-legged will move into the next Medicine Wheel blanketed in spirit, leaving the physical shell behind to nurture the Earth Mother. In this way we assist the Planetary Mother in birthing new plants. This then becomes the first Rite of Passage, birth, for the seeds of the Plant Tribe.

All life changes can be seen as painful or joyous. We decide whether we are going to respect our self-created process and capture the beauty along the way. The Rites of Passage card is the constant reminder to be grateful for the blessing of beauty in every moment of life. It may be time to ask yourself if you have noticed any changes in your desires or attitudes. Do you feel more creative? Do you want to spend more time with a special friend or more time alone doing inner work? Have your perceptions about life or people shifted recently? Has new commitment to a project suddenly appeared? Have you felt more at home with who you are? Are you restless and ready to move or travel? All of these feelings mark times of change. Notice how these shifts are occurring in your life and honor each new opening. When you notice and acknowledge the changes, your personal growth process is consciously available to you. With the conscious understanding of *how* you are changing, you are then able to monitor or alter your timing, decisions, and patterns of growth in order to receive the most rewards from every step you take.

In all cases, the Rites of Passage that mark our journeys on the Good Red Road signal changes in the way we grow, the way we use the wisdom of the lessons along the way, and the attitudes we choose that eventually create and shape our reality.

22

Heyokah

HUMOR/OPPOSITES

ATTRIBUTES
Learning through laughter • Accepting contrary lessons
• Tricking the Self into growth and knowledge • Healing through irreverence •
Having fun and being playful

CHALLENGES
Being too serious • Joking with no intent to harm • Being a good sport
• Tricking the ego into dropping self-importance • Working with the shadow-self •

Individual Applications

If the Heyokah has appeared on the scene, get ready to laugh. You have called in the Divine Trickster for a reason. If you are being stubborn and refusing to allow yourself unlimited alternatives when making decisions, you have called Heyokah to bust the stranglehold of your own attachments.

The Heyokah comes to teach us the value of clowning around and being playful or childlike again. The Heyokah points to other paths that lead to our goals but are unexpected and out of the ordinary. The tunnel vision that keeps us from exploring uncharted territory is one of Heyokah's targets. If in our seriousness, we cannot see the forest for the trees, Heyokah comes to tie us to a hot air balloon that takes us to the other side of the mountain. The balloon may pop on the way, dropping us in a swamp where we meet our fears, find our strengths, and conquer our self-imposed limitations. When we arrive at our goal, triumphantly covered with muck and mire, it is the Heyokah who greets us, laughing his head off. Then we can review the silly path we insisted on taking in order to grow and laugh with the Trickster, vowing never to be so stubborn again.

If life has become too heavy and you are taking on the problems of others, you are probably blocking your own creativity. *Stop it!* Just who told you that you had been appointed the world's messiah from Des Moines or wherever you are from? You better laugh at yourself before you become the self-appointed rescuer of the neighborhood. If you take away the ability of others to handle their own problems, you will learn a hard, contrary lesson when those being rescued resent you. Then it will be no laughing matter. The cure is to laugh at the reasons why you insist on rescuing others. Is it so you won't have to look at your own garbage or smell the unmistakable odor of your own fear?

Opposites attract or so the saying goes. The strong are attracted to the weak. Is it because it makes the strong feel needed or the weak feel taken care of and safe to continue being weak? In every set of opposites, there are many humorous lessons to be learned if we can find our hidden motives, which always reside in the shadow of self-importance. The decision that we no longer need those identities that hold our own projections can be easily made through humor. If we refuse to laugh at our projections of ourselves and others, we will then insist in all seriousness, to experience our contrary lessons that will bust us from behind, Heyokah-style.

Throwing away limitations through laughter is well worth the effort when the alternatives are viewed and followed by personal experience. The reality that challenges us daily is tied to our ability to find the power of humor as healers. Being human is a collective experience that holds unlimited possibilities. We are often at our best when things are at their worst. We find joy in the laughter that sets us free of our inhibitions. We mirror our problems and seriousness to each other in order to find new answers. When we can use mirrors to break our illusions instead of blaming our projections on others, we will have discovered the healing that comes from the Divine Trickster.

Ask yourself if you ever gave away your power. If you have, then laugh about it. The truth is that it is impossible to have power taken away or stolen. How can you steal another person's talent? How can anybody take away the abilities the Great Mystery gave you? Heyokah laughs at your perplexity and shows you how to turn the tables by seeing that you may have played the ultimate cosmic joke on yourself by buying into the "giving away your power" lie. You may have given your authority or self-esteem away for a moment, but that is not your power.

In all instances, Heyokah asks you to look at learning through the exact opposite of what you are now being, doing, or having. This slippery little Trickster wants you to see the cosmic joke in your present situation. Remember that the Heyokah never attacks *you,* the true Self, but he will attack your self-importance and your serious attempts to be anything that could limit the true potential you already carry, even if you have spent a lifetime hiding it from yourself. That is the cosmic joke. Now you have to hunt for the golden egg of your potential, which is most likely hidden in the pile of masks you have been using to disguise the true Self.

23

Smoke Signals

INTENT

ATTRIBUTES
Focus/aim • Working with purpose and perspective • Employing drive and ambition
• Using single-mindedness • Living with conviction and decisiveness •

CHALLENGES
Making no goals,having no aims • Never completing or mastering a lesson
• Fearing to create an effect • Having too many irons in the fire •
Having no interest or focal point

Individual Applications

The Smoke Signals in the Sky Nation are calling for you to notice the faces of the Cloud People. Look skyward and see the Medicine Helpers who appear in the clouds to ease your troubled heart or weary mind. Confusion and frustration are quelled when your heart hears the whispers of your personal Allies. These are the Guardians who can assist you in clearing away the confusion in order to restore your clear intent. Move past the smokescreen and aim high now.

It may be time to state your true intentions about discovering your personal truth. Without a purpose, the Pathfinder inside you has no direction or too many directions. Lack of direction can cause frustration or self-delusion. When you have admitted to yourself exactly why you are following a certain path, it may be easier to follow that path to completion, ensuring wisdom or mastery. On the other hand, you may choose to change your course or to acknowledge that an another person's intention has influenced your choices. If you have played follow the leader in order to be admired or accepted, stop. Look now at how that choice has affected your life and re-instill your heart's true desire. You may choose to make a list of the actions you have taken that involved the intentions of others. Then write down how those actions have added confusion to your original intent.

The Smoke Signals card may also be a type of warning flag marking the life signals that will keep you from following a crooked trail. If your intent is clear, you may need to watch the actions of others rather than believing their words. The web of confusion is often woven when we depend upon others who talk a good game but demonstrate nothing.

Another message of Smoke Signals is strictly personal. It may be time to examine the signals you are sending to others with your words or actions. Do you talk about your intentions yet lack the strength to follow through? If so, call upon the Allies by sending your prayers, through Smoke, to the Sky Nation. Observe the sky and the changes in the Clouds, the Creature-beings who enter your space while you are watching, and be sure to listen with your heart.

If you have lost the desire to master a challenge or if your aim has no drive or ambition behind it, you might want to apply the Fire Medicine card to the situation. The connection to the inner child has been severed if you have lost trust in your ability to create an effect on the world that would please you. You may want to apply the lessons of the South Shield card to the lack of faith you have in your ability to carry through on your intent. If you are wanting to go two directions at once, it may be time to make decisions by using the lessons of the Council Fire card. There is always a solution to the challenge of purifying your intent. Pick another card as an indicator that will tell you the Medicine needed to make your intent purposeful and decisive. Then focus on using your new single-mindedness to meet and to master the challenges in your present path.

In all cases, Smoke Signals is asking you to be clear and focused. Find the truth in every situation and insist that the beauty of your individual talents be given a chance to live and grow inside that truth. The original intent of Great Mystery was to create beauty that would live in truth and harmony with all other parts of the whole. In this manner, there is no need for imitation or envy. Every part of Creation has a separate intent and goal that will feed the whole. All life-forms have aimed their Arrows toward their targeted goals of wholeness. A sure course for each person is assured if the intent is pure. All of Creation has a common intent, which is to grow and evolve. Each part of Creation expresses that aim through the personal right to *be*. Intent creates cause and is followed by action. The result of that action produces effect. We are asked to be mindful of the effects we create in our world, knowing full well that those effects are products of our original intent.

24

Council Fire

DECISIONS

ATTRIBUTES
Decision—the first step to action • Ending indecision or confusion
• Coming to terms with truth • Taking charge of your life • Desiring a solution •
Honoring your right to be

CHALLENGES
Deciding to risk movement • Taking a chance
• Being willing to accept resolutions • Meeting opportunity •
Letting go of turmoil • Not giving in to doubt or the "what if's"

Individual Applications

To apply the Council Fire card to life, we must look at how to make decisions that will benefit everyone. Such decisions can almost always be achieved through negotiation or concessions. Compromises, which allow all concerned to feel that they received something, are always better than indecision, which can leave unresolved issues. If you drew this card, you are in need of making a firm decision about the situation now facing you. The steps for a personal decision are different from those needed to make a decision that will affect a group.

For a personal decision these steps may be helpful. Ask yourself the following questions:

What are my options? (List all of them.)

Am I following my heart by making this decision or am I doing it out of duty? Will this decision continue to make me happy in the future?

Do I need to rid myself of the fear of change or failure?

Will this decision allow me to further develop my talents?

Am I willing to be true to myself and carry this decision through with actions that will bring it to fruition?

For a decision that will affect the lives of others, these questions may be useful:

What are the possibilities or alternatives surrounding this decision? (List all of them.)

Have the opinions of all people involved been heard?

How will this decision affect this group in the future?

Are the needs of the greater portion of the whole going to be met by the solution to the situation? If so, what concessions can be given to others?

Are the opinions of a few influencing the decision for the whole?

Has the truth been found, and is the probable decision fair for everyone?

Am I willing to live by the same decisions I expect others to live by?

In all situations, the key to making proper decisions is total honesty. If we fool ourselves by deciding or volunteering to do something that others expect of us without feeling a true desire to do so, we will botch the job, resent the consequences, or procrastinate until it is long past time to complete the action. This is one example of why we get exhausted or apathetic when we are having to use effort to get a job done. We have lost the joy and the desire.

Desire is the first step of creation and when it is followed by a decision, that is the first step to taking action. The actions to make the decision manifest then become effortless. We must first desire to change the present situation enough to make a firm decision. There is nothing more maddening than a doubter who changes decisions as quickly as the wind changes direction. In this instance, all energy that has been mounting to physically effect a change is suddenly diverted to another area. When the energy is diverted and there is no clear-cut goal in sight, it dissipates and is suddenly consumed by any other strong, magnetic cause in the Spirit World. The energy moves to the stronger cause in order to create an effect in the universal growth patterns of the world.

In all cases, the Council Fire card reflects the decision *to be,* which was the first decision any life-form ever made. All decisions support our right to be. We should take care in decision making because we begin new creation processes every time we make one. We may even carry other life decisions from the past into our present paths. Changing old decisions is one way to clean up our Sacred Spaces. We do not need to live by negative decisions that are thought but not spoken. These unspoken relics of the past carry as much energy as we give them through our thoughts and actions. As we catch those thoughts and change them, we free our ability to make and carry out the decisions that shape our right *to be* in the here and now.

25

Pow-Wow

SHARING/QUICKENING

ATTRIBUTES
Sharing abilities, goods, and experiences • Preparing for awakening
• Feeling life quicken inside you • Mounting excitement. • Building energy •
Preparing for rebirth

CHALLENGES
Preparing properly • Dropping all expectations • Risking sharing
• Opening to new experience • Removing fear of the future • Stopping all projections •

Individual Applications

If you have chosen the Pow-Wow card, you may be called upon to gather friends together to share and celebrate life. New life is bursting inside you as you dance the moment of new awakening. You are preparing for a magical moment when life takes you beyond your present state of being.

In another situation, Pow-Wow may be pointing out that you have failed to gather the energy you need to prepare for this time of new awakening. It could come from your refusal to ask for help. Then again, it could come from your fear of asking for help and being refused. If the latter case is true, it is time to re-evaluate the people you have chosen as friends or acquaintances. Examine whether you have been supporting others by being neighborly. See if that feeling is shared. Do others come to your aid when you are in need? If this is not the case, it may be time to refill your life with people of substance who aren't trying to *be somebody* but rather find joy in naturally being themselves. Look at the true characters of those with whom you choose to share life and see exactly which qualities you respect in each of them.

All in all, the Pow-Wow card asks you to listen to the Pow-Wow drums and dance your preparation for the future. We can find joy in every life situation if we have gathered all of our Coup Sticks into one bundle, sharing our common victories as one. Tomorrow will always look dismal if we have forgotten to gather the gifts we have today. Have a Pow-Wow with yourself and gather your blessings, then toss out the doubt and fear that would rob every stick in your bundle if you gave it the chance. Stand at the outer rim of your Sacred Space and turn inward. Then make war upon the elements that you find in the doubting-self that would leak the energy you have gathered in preparation for the rebirth you are about to experience.

The Pow-Wow dancer dances a warning to drop all expectations and projections that could rob the future of unlimited potential. The perseverance to dance throughout the night in vigil keeps the mind at rest as the body takes over and dances the potential dream. The energy builds and is shared and recycled as the quickening begins within.

The key of the Pow-Wow card is the quickening. The quickening is the time before birth when new life builds inside you and can be felt moving about. As mother-to-be, you become aware of your child's intention to come alive inside of you. Your preparation time is nearing an end and you are being asked to celebrate the gestation time before birth. To acknowledge this time of quickening you are asked to make sure that you have your house in order and are ready for the labor of birth. The labor in this case is easy if the preparations are in order. You have shared your excitement with those who seek your joy as their own. You have built the energy within you in order to carry you into your next step. You have destroyed the doubts and fears with love. The child within you is nurtured and safe. You have done your homework and are ready for the joyous explosion of new life that is crying to become your manifested dream.

Your true family and friends are sharing your joy as the quickening takes hold and catapults you into the next state of awareness. This is the inner knowing that you are about to be reborn. Mark the time well and feel the joy of pregnancy. Whether you are male or female, this time is akin to the moment just before completion when you know that you are going to go over the edge of limitation and become the dream.

In all cases, Pow Wow signals that the energy is building, the excitement is mounting, and you are being asked to feel those emotions and currents of life within you. When you honor those feelings by being aware of them, they can be shared and funneled into further creativity. Stay with each new wave of life-force being taken in by your body and feel the glory of being alive!

26

Warbonnet

ADVANCE

ATTRIBUTES
Moving forward • Taking action in a positive way • Charging ahead!
• Exhibiting a confident willingness to be a pathfinder • Exploring the new •

CHALLENGES
Letting go of the comfort of old habit patterns • Leaping forward with faith
• Fearing the future • Refusing to take right action • Lacking boldness or courage •

Individual Applications

The Warbonnet card asks each of us to look at how we view advancement. In Native American teachings we understand that unless everyone does well, no one does well. This may be a hard pill to swallow in the modern world, but it is a necessary cure for the state of planetary awareness today.

What if the world powers called a war and nobody came? What if you just decided that you were going to sidestep any activity that hurt the Earth Mother or her children? That could be a form of spiritual advancement, couldn't it? It would certainly change your awareness. This is not to say that you should try and force others to go along with you. Warbonneted Chiefs would not follow others or insist that others follow them. All Tribal Members were allowed to follow their own Paths of Beauty.

The Warbonnet card may bring you understanding of your Warrior-nature, your courage. This is always the forerunner to the real issue, which is acknowledging the gifts you can share with the Children of Earth. Warbonnet may be showing you how to advance or develop those qualities within the Self that you have been afraid to use. If you lack trust in the Self, the potential for leadership or success can be frightening.

Another message of this card is that if you have been indecisive about some area of your life, now is the time to advance. Call upon all your Medicine Helpers and get with it! Use the counsel of those Allies so that the signs become clear and then follow your heart. You will never know the victory of Counting

Coup if you don't try. The worst thing that could happen is that you could fall on your face. So what? Persistence is the sign of the male and female Warriors. The Coup Feather at the end of the line may be the goal you have always wanted to accomplish. Advance now!

If you feel that none of these messages apply, look at this hidden signal that the Warbonnet brings. The past is behind you. The trail before you has many detours if you are fearful. The courage it takes to make it to your next level of experience should always be balanced with good judgment, patience, selflessness, wise counsel, and assistance from the Medicine Helpers and Great Mystery. The manner in which you use these talents will shape your destiny. To fulfill your destiny, you must climb the feather ladder of the Warbonnet and own your setbacks as well as your Coups. Balanced moods, actions, desires, and goals are the true tests of a Warbonneted Chief.

You are the only person who can find what is necessary for growth in your life. To do this you must remove the blockages, negative thoughts, or doubts. Trust the strength within you and enjoy the freedom that Eagle offers through the feathers of the Warbonnet. Declare war on the pettiness in your world, not through anger, but through loving yourself enough to live your truth with compassionate understanding for those who do not walk your same path. They may not change but *you* will. You can lead through example by using truth and courage.

In all cases, the Warbonnet calls upon your inner resources and willingness to do something about your present situation. You have been given a green light and are being forced to ask yourself the question, "Am I willing to be a pathfinder and to explore the possibilities of my future creations by boldly taking action now?" Since the green light has been given through drawing this card, the only barrier to advancement would be your refusal to acknowledge the strength you have within. Be assured that if action is taken in the here and now, one of the rewards of that advancement will be more self-confidence in the future.

27

Cradleboard

ABILITY TO RESPOND

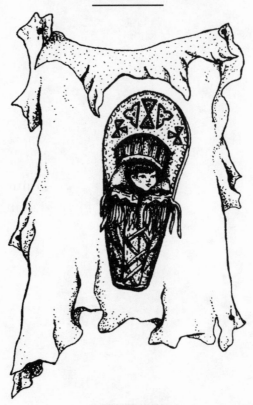

ATTRIBUTES

Acting on feelings or personal truth • Responding to your own talents or abilities
• Acknowledging opportunity • Answering the call of the here and now •
Being fully present • Understanding the situation and taking your role in it

CHALLENGES

Letting others respond for you • Feeling apathy • Refusing to take charge
• Doing nothing • Ignoring your talents •
Responding too late or not at all because of doubt

Individual Applications

The Cradleboard card can mark a time of noticing how you respond to life. Do you react without thinking or feeling? Do you seek the wisdom of that which will assist the future seven generations when making decisions? Is the adult part of you nurturing and protecting the child within you?

In all cases the Cradleboard card is calling you to respond to some new creation in your life that will affect the future of the next seven generations. This could become confusing since most people do not feel that anything they create is going to change the world. Whether or not we use biodegradable soap affects the Earth Mother's ability to keep water clean for drinking. Recycling cans and glass will affect the future. Cleaning up the litter in a park affects the future. Teaching our children that *more is not always better* will help them formulate new ideas in their generation. Talking rather than screaming will change how our children will relate to one another. Asking questions without shame will open hearts and minds to new ideas. Helping others to rid themselves of guilt created by old belief systems will create a natural, loving world to come.

If you are looking at how to respond to some area of your life—a new idea, a decision, a new person, or new interest—the Cradleboard card asks you to respond with joy. Each new experience can bring an opportunity to learn a new set of lessons about the Self. Adaptability and willingness to experience life with joy will stop you from experiencing fear and the hard knocks that inflexibility brings. Although the Cradleboard protects the baby from harm's way, it is flexible enough to fall without splintering and it is cushioned enough to protect the child within. Trust that you will respond correctly to any life situation without panic and know that you are responding to the all-powerful Great Mystery who lives within you.

Response in any situation can have its challenges. Have you failed to speak up and then cringed when others have answered for you? Have you felt that life or opportunity has passed you by because you could not be responsible and act on your feelings? Possibly doubt has been the limitation that has haunted your path to wholeness. If any of these statements apply to your situation, it is time to look at the challenges to learning this lesson and begin to remove them.

Our ability to respond to life is dependent upon our willingness to be in the here and now. If we are not willing to fall on our faces from time to time, we have excused ourselves from the learning process. If we have some hidden feeling that prevents us from being humble students of life, we have lost the cutting edge that allows our actions to be noticed as unique and full of courage. Our talents cannot be used unless we respond to the steps that hone those skills into shining Arrows tipped with diamondlike cutting edges. We can pierce the veil of self-importance and fear if we are willing to respond to the opportunities life brings.

Even when our experiences are unhappy or uncomfortable, we are being given the opportunity to respond to them through learning. If we see each task as an opportunity to learn or be of service we will have bested the doubt within our critical selves. When our shadows insist that we are too good for an activity, we are losing an opportunity to learn humility. When we refuse to respond to an opportunity by judging it before we get the facts, we are often masking our fear in order to be safe. The masks of our fears often take the form of boredom or apathy. In all instances, the Cradleboard asks us to check with the child within and allow the wonder of life to be our guide. In being totally present we become the here and now.

28

Medicine Bundle

ALLIES/SUPPORT

ATTRIBUTES
Accepting assistance • Asking for what you need
• Acknowledging the Allies and the support given • Showing appreciation •
Honoring your personal Medicine and that of others

CHALLENGES
Becoming willing to receive
• Showing willingness to support others with the choices they make •
Listening to your heart • Willing to be true to the Self
• Following through when you have been supported •

Individual Applications

If you have chosen the Medicine Bundle card, you are being asked to find a Medicine for your present situation. If you need courage to face the future, you should call upon Great Mystery and nature's helpers to answer your prayer. Then see which Medicine or omen the Allies send you. If this Medicine serves you well, you may want to find an object that represents that strength or ability to you and add it to your personal bundle or pouch.

In picking the Medicine Bundle card, you may be sending yourself a message that you are in need of reclaiming a certain ability, strength, courage, talent, or connection. Close your eyes for a moment and imagine which Creature-being in nature has the ability you seek. Call upon that friend to teach you about yourself. Allow that Ally to guide you to the place in your heart where you have hidden your talent or strength. Then breathe into that space and allow the feeling or the essence of that gift to be received by you. Reclaim the gift you received by making a decision to respect the spirit who has aided you. Then continue your new relationship with this Ally by giving permission for further lessons to come to you in the form of experiences, dreams, or visions. Invite the energy of the Ally into your life and honor the instruction by following the guidance.

In all cases, this card is a reminder of the vast world of Creatures, Stone People, Ancestors, Standing People (trees), Winged-Ones, Finned-Ones, Creepy-crawlers (insects), and natural elements that are ready to assist you. These Allies stand to gain as well. In coming into harmony with their essences, we may once again create a world that is a paradise of peace. You must always ask the Allies for assistance, thereby giving them your permission to be of aid. So this card can also be a reminder to ask. You may already have some Medicine talent you are not using, and if this is so, this card is a reminder to review the items or Totems that have aided you in the past. The Ancestors also fall into this category and are a part of the World of Spirit that is available to lend a hand.

The support you seek from the Allies of nature is a gift of the Great Mystery. This support is freely given with love. The duty of anyone receiving support is to use it properly and to share its rewards with others. The seeker who listens to advice and ignores the gift given is not deserving of support and on some level does not honor the Self. The projection is evident: when one does not trust the answers within, the answers from others are also not to be trusted.

When a magical moment is present in our lives, some kind of alliance is being made. This alliance can be a connection to the Original Source, one's Self, another person, the life-force, the Earth Mother, or anything in the universe. The Allies are those Guardians who assist us in making new alliances with all life-forms and forces. Our support systems are built on an interdependence that is based in love and truth. When we reach for the stars and find the loving support of those who want for us what we want for ourselves, we have come to understand the full truth of Great Mystery's support for all of Creation. The Medicine Bundle is the symbol of our support system, which physically mirrors and reminds us of the support and love being sent our way from Great Mystery and all of Creation.

If you have never made a Medicine Bundle, it may be time to begin if you receive this card. (See p. 218 of the *Sacred Path*

Cards™ book for instructions.) If you have chosen this card for no other reason, you are being asked to reconnect with those Allies who are assisting your Earth Walk and to acknowledge your assets and gifts. With Great Mystery's support for your personal Medicine or ability to heal the Self, you will always win.

29

Storyteller

EXPANSION

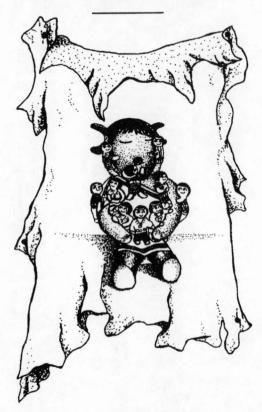

ATTRIBUTES
Increasing borders • Opening/growth of Self • Finding new interests
• Commanding more Sacred Space • Reaching for new experience •
Stretching beyond former capacity for living • Integrating new horizons

CHALLENGES
Contracting • Fearing new experience
• Expanding too fast without learning the steps • Losing control •
Needing to control your own growth • Wanting authority instead of growth

Individual Applications

If the Storyteller card has appeared in your spread today, you are being asked to listen to the words of others and apply their experiences to your life in order to expand your experience. The wisdom of knowing that crooked trails lead others astray and that happy trails bring enrichment can save you time when making your own decisions. An expanded viewpoint can give you many new alternatives and options to enhance your growth potential. The wise listener does not need to fall from Horse in order to understand that the ground is hard. The fall from authority can be hard and can hurt. Expanding beyond the point of present understanding can create a fall that reminds the one falling that expansion without knowing is futile.

The Storyteller card also asks you to share your hard-learned lessons and experiences with others if you see them walking a crooked trail or making a decision that will cause them pain. The idea is to share what happened to you rather than to point a finger at their decisions. Then allow them to discern what is right for them in their own way. Only Great Mystery knows why a crooked path could be of benefit to a person. You can only provide alternatives for others through sharing what you experienced in similar situations. Allowing each person to make the decisions that will be right for her or him is one way to ensure growth.

In all cases, the Storyteller card is asking us to keep the love of life alive. Whether through recounting stories that allow others a basis for introspection or through bringing news of another's victories, the Storyteller inside of you can bring the excitement of being alive to any situation. Each of us is a bridge to new understanding. We can remind friends of happy memories if they are feeling down. We can share an exciting idea and give birth to creativity. We can speak from our hearts and show others our appreciation. We can spin a tale that brings new insight and purpose to those who have forgotten how to weave their dreams. In every instance, the caring and sharing of the Twisted Hair or Storyteller is one way to remind ourselves and others that the future lives in us now.

We can expand our experience, our circle of friends, our sense of Self, our knowing, our talents, our ability to love, our roles in life, our ability to respond, our sphere of influence, our blessings, and every act of living through listening and applying the truth. This expansion can come in unlimited ways when we open ourselves to it. When we choose to resist the growth that comes our way, we do not hold the space we have, we contract. This contraction comes from the resistance we allow in our Sacred Spaces. The resistance magnetizes doubts and fears and brings these shadows into our personal Medicine Wheels. The result is usually painful growth into the next phase of life. We continue to grow but we fight it every inch of the way. We refuse to listen to the expansive Self who is being our teacher and who tells the story of our passage.

The Storyteller card always asks us to stretch beyond our former capacity and to be the creators of our own Medicine Stories. Each experience told and retold will assist another in applying it to his or her life. The need to control the story as we are walking it stops the natural expansion process. There can be no stretching or adventure when we know exactly what to expect at every turn. The beauty of surprise endings is left in the mud of sticky control issues when we project how we are going to grow, at what rate, with whom, and under which circumstances. The adventure of surprising expansion is the gift. The question is whether we are willing to walk through every step of learning in order to earn the right to command the new expanded space we are growing into.

30

Fire Medicine

PASSION/SPONTANEITY

ATTRIBUTES

Having zest for life • Desiring to live life to the fullest
• Expressing without hindrance • Acting in a timely fashion •
Showing vigor, warmth, responsiveness, creativity • Embracing the life-force

CHALLENGES

Wanting to be someone else or elsewhere • Finding the ecstasy of being alive
• Banishing coldness, numbness, and lack of passion •
Dropping boredom or apathy • Fearing our own fiery nature

Individual Applications

If Fire has burned its way into your cards today, take heed, you may have grown cold or uncaring of your body, your friends, your lover, mate, or a family member. If this is the case, take time and bring in Mother Earth's Fire to burn away your lack of compassion. Lack of compassion can signal a time of pushing the Self too hard and then projecting that hardheadedness onto others. The natural passion for living, in this case, is smothered by an unhealthy drive to accomplish too much.

On another level, Fire Medicine may be telling you that you are in need of warmth, human caring, or sexual intimacy. Have you honored your personal need to be with those who support your present path? Have you allowed yourself to be hugged by a friend? Are your attitudes about sexual release or fear of being unworthy of pleasure stopping you from feeling complete when you make love? Do you need to release old fears or guilt regarding sexuality? If any of these questions apply to your present situation, it is time to use the breath to release and clear the old thought patterns so that you may create a space for receiving the joy of a mate, love from friends, warmth in your own heart, or the feeling of being connected to others. To do this you must start by being loving and merciful toward the Self.

Fire Medicine can also be a red flag pointing to physical exhaustion or some small illness that nags you at times. This is a probable sign that you need sunshine, fresh air, a feeling of reconnection to the Earth Mother so that her warmth may feed your stamina. A lack of exercise can stop the internal flame in our bodies from burning away bacteria. When we exercise, our bodies naturally heat up and the inner Fire flushes out toxins through perspiration. Our breath feeds that inner Fire and we breathe more when we exercise. We draw our internal Fire through Mother Earth by being physical and allowing our bodies to make connection with the soil beneath us. This flow or energy exchange is why Indian Runners were always at one with the Earth yet a part of the Wind. The physical activity keeps us healthy and fires our internal Sun.

If you are trying to do some Journey Work or meditation, this card may be a reminder to use the Fire Medicine to keep your body in tune while your Spirit journeys. Candles may be used to draw life-force into the body if you are in a place where a fire would not be possible. Practice breathing the Fire Medicine into your body and give the body permission to draw warmth from the flames as well as fiery connection from the Mother Earth while you are journeying. Breathe deeply and hold your breath briefly while tightening your hip muscles, then exhale. This will fan the fire within.

Fire Medicine comes from the joining of Grandfather Sun and the Earth Mother's molten core or heart. The product of Divine Union is called the Eternal Flame. We receive our creativity and life-force from this union and the reflection of our own inner Divine Union of male and female. We lack boldness, spontaneity, fervor, and desire to create when we have shut the door on the fire within. Inhibition of our natural desire to create and live life to the fullest can lead to guilt, boredom, fear, apathy, and feeling dead.

In all cases, the Fire Medicine card is speaking of balancing the spark of Creation within you that feeds your creativity. Use your creativity and master the blockages to your receiving light and spiritual food from Great Mystery, Mother Earth, and Grandfather

Sun. Then in turn, share the Fire inside you with others by burning away ideas of separation and creating bridges that speak of our similarities. Spontaneous combustion is the internal feeling of raw creativity and passion for being alive. Through Fire we rise from the ashes of our beingness into the regenerated Self that becomes at one with the Eternal Flame, which is our common supply of life-force. With that life-force we can move mountains and be our dreams. Reclaiming the Fire is the way we reclaim the love we have forgotten to feel. The only pain we take to the Spirit World is love we refused to feel and share here on Earth.

31

Medicine Bowl

HEALING

ATTRIBUTES
Returning to the womb to seek healing • Questioning the Void
• Using answers found to effect cures •
Using your healing abilities • Being willing to feel

CHALLENGES
Healing the Self • Fearing the Void or the unknown
• Honoring your feeling/healing process • Owning your ability to heal the Self •
Trusting your visions and the Allies who assist you

Individual Applications

If the Medicine Bowl card has shown up in your spread today, it may signal a time of developing your knowledge of herbal remedies or knowledge of plants in the wild. If you have had an interest in this area before, now is the time to begin your study of herbs or wild, edible foods.

If you have not been interested in learning about healing plants, it may be time for another area of development such as learning to develop your gifts of intuition, seeing, hearing, and observation. Ask yourself, when was the last time that you remembered all that was said in a conversation? How are you using your gift of intuition? Can you observe and remember detail? Can you trust your feelings? Have you ever felt the presence of a Totem Animal or Ancestor trying to communicate with you?

It may be time for you to try the Medicine Bowl exercise of seeking answers described in the *Sacred Path Card™* book (p. 240). Be sure to use a blackened bowl and never use it for another purpose after you use it as a Seer's Medicine Bowl.

If you do not feel that any of the other messages of this card apply, the general meaning is that in some area of your life there is a need for healing. Ask yourself the following questions:

Are my thoughts positive and focused? If not, use some
sage smoke to clear your thinking.

Am I physically tired? Am I bored? Ask yourself if you
need a change in situation, a new job, a new goal,

fresher foods, more exercise, or a change in attitude. If you answered yes, call one of your Totem Animals to assist you in seeking which type of healing is best at this time.

Do I need new answers to my present situation? Ask whether you should seek a vision in a blackened Medicine Bowl or whether you merely need to Enter the Silence and watch for the answers to appear in your life.

In answering these questions, know that if you are not ready or open to the answers or visions, they will not come. The fear of the future or the unknown is its own protective device. Until we have healed our fear and replaced it with trust and faith, no clear answers will come and our own doubt will prevail. To heal the doubt in our lives is to fully trust our roles in Great Mystery's flawless plan. Learning to use a Medicine Bowl may be the first step in trusting the Medicine Allies and the answers received. In this manner each of us achieves personal healing. As always, every step of any seeking ceremony is accompanied by prayers of gratitude and songs of joy or praise. Use songs you have heard or create your own.

Remember, the Medicine Bowl card is the symbol of healing. If you feel healed, then teach or share how you were healed with others who ask for assistance. Never give information or assistance that has not been asked for or wanted by another. Be still and listen if you have asked for information from another. Always use any Teaching or Medicine for the highest good of all concerned. These rules are part of a Code of Honor used by Women Seers who use the Medicine Bowl to assist others in healing their lives.

In all instances the Medicine Bowl reminds us of the healing that is being held in the womb of the Earth Mother, waiting for birth. To receive that healing we must go to our planetary

Mother and ask to be healed. Then it is necessary for us to trust the healing process as Mother Earth manifests it in our lives by giving it life. We assist this birthing process by eliminating the barriers to our healing. With each contraction, our common labor brings challenges to our healing process. In besting those challenges, we release the wounded child and birth a new aspect of ourselves that represents the healed healer within us. This is the magic of the Earth Mother's womb, which took form as the Medicine Bowl in the Lodge of the Clan Mothers.

32

Drum

RHYTHM/INTERNAL TIMING

ATTRIBUTES
Signifying Earth Mother's heartbeat • Being in sync with life
• Feeling the beat • Finding your rhythms • Using proper timing or cycles •
Knowing when and how

CHALLENGES
Listening/feeling • Trusting the body's rhythms • Being on a schedule
• Hearing your heart's desire • Making time for what is really important •
Being in the here and now

Individual Applications

If the beat of the Drum has spoken to you today, you may be asked to discover if you are out of step with your body's natural rhythm. Examine whether you have recently taken the time to get in sync with those patterns that allow your body to find its own rhythm without being pushed by you. If your body functions are not regular and your energy is low, this is a sure clue that you and your body are not working as a team.

If everything you are trying to accomplish is just a matter of trying rather than actual doing, it is time to see what is causing your heart, mind, and spirit to be out of sync. If you are forcing yourself to move faster than your natural rhythm, it is time to stop, take a breath, relax, and find the natural rhythm again before attempting anything else. Time is an illusion but *timing is everything*. The heartbeat of Creation calls us to know how and when to ride the waves of our feelings into victorious living. In feeling the rhythm and cycles of the rest of Creation, we may better use the combined energy of the whole to Count Coup on our limitations.

If you are at odds with yourself or another at this time, perhaps you are hearing the beat of a different drummer. Trying to force yourself to do something you don't really want to do is a sure way to get stuck in the quicksand of denying your right to express your creativity and uniqueness. This is the crooked trail that keeps the Children of Earth in bondage. To fully use your gifts for the greater good, you must first listen to the beat of your own heart. The key to finding your place in Creation and joyfully completing these tasks is in learning to *feel* what is right for you.

Another message of Drum speaks of the need to reconnect with the heartbeat of the Earth Mother. Does your inner child remember the warmth and safety of the first sound your ears heard? If not, that sound was your Mother's heartbeat melding with your own. This memory can be recreated by using the Drum and listening to your heartbeat while beating out another lub-dub, lub-dub rhythm. Continue the beat until you feel safe and reconnected to the Earth Mother and all of her children.

Drum also talks to our hearts about other realities and parallel universes. Drum reminds us that we must maintain our connection to the Earth in order to sustain our bodies if we intend to Journey out-of-body. Safe return is insured if the Drumbeat is used as a map or blueprint. In this way, the first sound of being physical ties us to the world of matter. Our bodies feel the rhythm, our hearts feel connection, and the patterns of sound make a road to come home by.

Remember that each individual creation has been given a rhythm by Great Mystery. These combined rhythms are the sum total of Creation. The Music of the Spheres is the music of the Sacred Hoop. This Circle will remain unbroken as long as each individual retains his or her own rhythm while allowing all others to do the same.

In all cases, Drum calls us to acknowledge our heart's desire and to follow the internal timing that allows us to know the cycles of Creation. These cycles speak to us of seasons, of knowing when to plant our desires and when to harvest. Every life-form has cycles of living and an internal feeling and knowing about when to use them. Two-leggeds can overcome their natural feeling of internal timing when they ignore their natural state of being and intellectualize life. Natural urges to dance, run, move, and play are the body's way of getting a tune-up. If we ignore these signals, we have lost our rhythms. The Drum is one way to manifest the internal rhythms so that we can hear them. The joy of reconnection is based on allowing every person to find her or his harmony to the melody of the Earth Mother's heartbeat. Nobody can think this rhythm, it has to be felt and experienced.

33

Dreamtime

UNLIMITED VISION

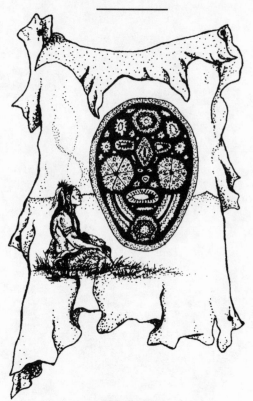

ATTRIBUTES

Observing the obvious • Opening all possibilities • Being at home in other realities
• Bridging all worlds • Acknowledging the potential dreamer within •
Having willingness to become your vision and be the dream
• Healing denial or blindness •

CHALLENGES

Clearing your eyes • Opening your experience for new ideas to enter
• Journeying farther than your experience allows • Dreaming a dream big enough •
Learning the paths to the Spirit World and using them wisely

Individual Applications

If you have chosen the Dreamtime card you are being asked to expand your awareness of what you perceive to be real. In limiting your reality to the physical world in front of your eyes, you are disallowing the other wonders that Great Mystery has created for your growth. If some of the Dreamtime experiences seem bizarre to you, ask yourself if you could imagine being inside a pond of water and knowing that you could breathe below it's surface. Do you remember having flying dreams as a child? Have you ever felt as if you know the location of a house or landmark in an area where you have never been before? If you answer yes to any of these questions, you have already experienced a little of the parallel Dreamtime reality.

Pulling the Dreamtime card is an omen that more of this reality is open to you if you choose to pursue it. It may be time to make a dream log and further examine your Sleeptime dreams. If you feel that you are a Dreamer, you may choose to study with a Shaman or Medicine Teacher. If you are already journeying out-of-body and are trained, you may be ready for further expeditions into the realms of bending physical law. This could be the ability to be in two places at one time physically and be aware of it. If this is your next step, call on Crow as your teacher. Crow is the shape-shifter of the waking dream.

The first step in acknowledging your capability to access the message the Dreamtime card has for you is to acknowledge that you chose this card for a reason. Obviously you are kicking your Self in the subconscious so that you can learn some sort of lesson that is multidimensional from another reality. It may be some subtle form of Self-exploration or it could be that you are opening to more fully understanding how all life interrelates. Whatever the reason, you are insisting that you grow beyond some limited concept that is keeping you tied in the bog of physical reality. This concept of journeying only applies to those who do not use it as an escape. On the other hand, for the skeptical, using Sleeptime dreams and seeking solutions to the daily challenges may be the next step.

If you have a hard time remembering your dreams, you may choose to make an Apache Dream Net or Dream Catcher. The Dream Net is made from a piece of Willow, the Wood of Love. It is about eight inches long when completed and is shaped like the number nine (9). In the circle at the top, you would make a Spider web from sinew or red string. The lines to the center should be evenly spaced and tied securely. It should have eight strings looking similar to the drawing of the Dream Weaver on p.197. Then weave the web from the outside to the center so that the dreams will be caught in Spider's web for you to remember. Place the Dream Net above your head in a horizontal position so that when you look up to the headboard of your bed, you see the web's pattern fully. The stem may be braced by placing it under something heavy or tied to the headboard for permanent use. The Dream Catcher is to allow you catch the Dreamtime Visions that permeate your sleep time and allow you the full use of this Good Medicine.

The Dreamtime card is also telling us that we have the ability to access our unconscious levels of thought, but we must begin by observing the obvious in the physical world. This ability to observe without denial may manifest in our lives in a multitude of ways: a new heart opening, a healing, a new direction, clearer perceptions, expanded understanding, and/or an explosion of awakening. In all instances, the Dreamtime card calls for the extraordinary on your part. Trust in your sense of observation and your sense of adventure to the degree that you are ready to experience life in *every* form and dimension available. *Remember, life is not always as it seems. Are you the Dreamer? Or are you the dreamed?*

34

Burden Basket

SELF-RELIANCE

ATTRIBUTES
Exhibiting strength of character and self-sufficiency • Taking care of business
• Being poised, confident • Handling life with ease • Having responsibility for self •
Using your gifts to the highest potential • Owning your mastery

CHALLENGES
Using own talents • Avoiding panic or running for help
• Not being a burden or victim • Refusing to carry another's burdens •
Procrastinating • Trusting who you are

Individual Applications

Burden Basket tells us that our strengths are not found in how many burdens we can carry, but rather in our ability to use that strength to toss those burdens into the Fire of Creation so that we may continue life by celebrating the joy of our present creations. When we sacrifice the sticky, old victim routine, we can look the future in the face. Then it will be time to weave a new Burden Basket that holds the different reflections of our burdens . . . our joy.

When we acknowledge our ability to create our own joy through self-reliance, we are trusting the Self. The poise and self-assuredness that accompanies this new sense of well-being is true balance. When we can drop the victim role in our shadow side and stand proud, we have learned how to carry our own burdens. When we let others do the same by refusing to always be there to rescue them, we have empowered them to find their own strengths.

Since the Burden Basket has appeared in your cards today both sides of this lesson apply. It could be time to rid yourself of some bit of gossip or worry you unwillingly added to the weight you are already carrying. If this does not seem to apply to your present situation, look and see if you have dumped your burdens on another without asking permission. Handle the problem if you feel it was unfair of you to add to their burdens by offering an apology. Do not add to your present lot by taking on any guilt. Simply forgive the error and correct the attitude that made you feel it was necessary to dump your problems on another. One way of correcting the attitude is to receive consent from friends before talking about your problems. Another way to handle the situation is to go within your own consciousness, in silence, and find the place where your personal answers live. Then access your truths by listening to the wise person that lives within you or the Elder you will become.

Another message of the Burden Basket may be that you are ignoring or not feeling the strength that lives inside of you. Weakness is really based upon an inability to make a decision. If we look at our weaknesses rather than our strengths, we are refusing the original decision we made *to be*. When Great Mystery created all things as thoughts and gave free will, we each had to make the decision to be physically manifest or not. It took great strength to decide to walk the Red Road of physical life. That strength has not disappeared except, perhaps, in our minds. Call upon the power of that original decision and feel again the strength to master any situation.

In another instance, the Burden Basket reveals the lessons of seeking counsel from a person more experienced or wiser. Never ask for assistance unless you intend to honor the advice being given. Always choose a person who has earned your respect and trust through actions, not words. Then be willing to listen and act upon the wisdom given. To refuse to heed the advice you have asked for because of your sense of self-importance, lack of faith, simple stubbornness, need to always be right, fear of failure, or unwillingness to try something new is foolish and immature. Remember to be grateful for the wisdom shared and to give back something for that wisdom. It can be some needed household item, a dinner out, money, flowers, or a thank you that you have personally chosen, but the return flow is needed to show that you respect the teacher or wise person who assisted your growth.

The Burden Basket always speaks of a time when you have the capacity to believe in your strength of character and to use your talents in order to achieve the self-reliance you seek. The independent action that leads you to greater heights is a sweet victory. By using your own steam to forge a new trail, you have risked and earned the right to be proud of who and what you are. This sense of well-being is something that no one can give you or take from you. The knowing that you have bested your burdens and made the shadow-self take notice is a rare and precious gift to the Self. You have now proven to the shadow that you have a right to be.

35

Shawl

RETURNING HOME

ATTRIBUTES
Rediscovering the home of the heart • Embracing and loving the true Self
• Coming back to the natural way of being • Reclaiming your truth •
Being secure in your balance and center • Owning the joy of life without denial

CHALLENGES
Finding happiness • Feeling at home everywhere • Knowing the true Self
• Having the courage to rediscover the places of the heart •
Dropping the masks of the pretender • Returning to live in truth

The Cards

Individual Applications

If you are in need of returning home, the Shawl may have appeared in you spread today. This could mean that you have lost your way or have lied to yourself about where your heart feels at home. If something you are doing or pretending to be is making you feel uncomfortable, there is a chance that your heart is troubled. If peer pressure or insistence from others has forced you into acting out an uncomfortable role, you need to re-evaluate the situation. The reason for walking a crooked trail is to experience what is right for you and what isn't. Your home is your heart. The road home may be long and difficult, but the rewards are far greater than you may imagine. The beauty of feeling good about yourself comes when you are living the truth instead of pretending. It may be time to state how you really feel. Then you may adopt a new method of relating to your personal truth when you drop the masks of denial.

Another message of the Shawl is that returning to a more natural way of life can make you feel happy and at one with the world. If you have gotten yourself caught in a situation where you are working more than you are living life, it may be time to see if the rat race is still serving your growth. If this applies to you, it may be time to look at how much you have given up in order to feel like you are a part of some peer group or income bracket. Ask your heart if all the trappings are worth the effort; then decide how you want to restructure your present situation.

The Shawl is also asking each person to seek the heart-place that allows him or her to honor the paths of others. In this fashion, the Shawl is showing us that all life-forms are examples of perfection that are expressed by every part of Creation. We need to trust the fact that Great Mystery has a Divine Plan. There is no need to mistrust anyone as long as we observe and use discernment. We may always trust each person to be exactly who and what they are at any given moment. Every person is unique and is evolving. We need not label one another or criticize the actions of others during this common growth process of physical life. When we return home to our center, it is easy to recognize those who would take advantage of or would harm others. Wasted energy used to rumor monger could be used to discover further celebration of life. If someone is trying to deceive you, don't waste your life-force by feeding their negativity. You are protected by the Shawl if you are Walking in Beauty. Recognize the envy or jealousy that created the need to harm another and then have compassion for them.

Remember that the freedom afforded by the Shawl is the home of truth and lives in harmony with All Our Relations. If you are at odds with your heart's purest desire, it is time to Take On the Shawl and come home to the arms of the Earth Mother. The willingness to grow and change the Self is always more comfortable when one is nurtured by the Earth Mother. Through laughter and tears every person has the right to heal and rediscover the Self.

The roles that we play in infinite Creation become our homes. From time to time there is a need for us to clean house and change those roles that make up our personal lodges. Some of us may have left the lodge of the true Self and lost our way back to it. The trail back home could be made of truth but littered with confusion. Some may have pitched a lodge made of fear that sits only a few feet from the road home, but their fear won't let them see it. Others could live in the cold heart lodge that keeps them behind walls, afraid to feel. The lodges situated far from the true homes of those who have wandered may be made of another's lies, forgetfulness, pain, loss, greed, bitterness, apathy, sloth, disconnection, faithlessness, or vanity. Any crooked trail that led the wanderers to live in those places can be set straight. The Earth Mother welcomes all of her wandering children to the place of rest and surrounds them with her Shawl of protection while they heal. If you have lost your way, the Shawl welcomes you home to the Self once again. Take courage and follow love back to your home of the heart.

36

Thunder-beings

USABLE ENERGY

ATTRIBUTES
Using life-force/creativity • Assets and abundance • Ideas and solutions
• Talents, abilities, and gifts • Persistence and tenacity •
Health/physical • Strength and stamina

CHALLENGES
Leaking energy • Accepting what is offered • Using available energy to create more
• Replenishing energy •Acknowledging the value of personal energy and health •

Individual Applications

The Thunder Beings are mighty teachers and issue in a time of renewed energy or creativity. Proper use of that energy is the ultimate lesson our Sky Nation friends can impart. Learning to ask for assistance and then being willing to use the energy received to "grow corn" in some facet of your daily life is the key to this card's lesson. The harvest you gather depends upon your readiness to plow the old habits into the soil in order to fertilize the seeds of the new direction you are taking.

To apply the Thunder-beings card, it is necessary to review all the types of energy available to you. (See the list under usable energy opposite.) By answering the following questions you may see exactly what type of energy offered by the Thunder-beings is available for use in your present situation.

Do you have the energy to maintain physical fitness?

Do you use your mental energy to solve the problems of others instead of assisting yourself in meeting your goals?

Do you use your physical energy during a day to accomplish needed actions?

Are you wasting life-force energy on worry, negativity, or procrastination?

Do you take time to renew your body's energy when you have put in long hours of effort?

Do you recognize the energy flows in your body and use
them properly or do you just push the body mentally
without honoring its needs?

Do you see money, time, emotions, actions, ideas, and
creativity as part of your available energy?

Do you hide your sexual energy or flow it improperly to
others who are already committed?

The Thunder-beings card calls to each of us in a different
way. We are being asked to evaluate the actions in our lives that
use energy. When we find answers that produce more creative
energy in our lives, we are asked to use the energy we gather from
those activities to enhance our happiness and balance. When we
no longer find joy in an activity, we are being asked to seek
renewal in another way.

The Thunder-beings speak of Divine Union, which in the
personal sense is the marriage of male and female within us. This
marriage creates usable energy or enhances our natural growth
potential by funding us with the get up and go we need to make
our dreams a reality. This card brings the message that usable
energy is now available for creation. Change the patterns that no
longer support right action.

The challenges of learning the lessons of the Thunder-
beings card are many. We must look at our assets and abilities as
pure energy instead of seeing them as actions or objects. As we
exchange energy with all other life-forms in our world the keynote
is balance. To give too much to others without replenishing the
self is imbalance. To take without returning gratitude or acknowledgment is imbalance. To spend more money than we produce by
our own creative efforts is imbalance. To wait for energy to come
to us without actively seeking what we need is imbalance. To leak
energy instead of using what is available is imbalance. To hoard
energy instead of circulating it is imbalance.

In all cases, the Thunderers send the Fire-sticks from the Sky Nation to shock us into feeling the energy that is available for creativity. The more creative we become, the more energy we will be funded. When we hoard, misuse, ignore, leak, or deny the energy coming our way, we are breaking the circle of creative life-force that naturally flows between us and the Original Source, Great Mystery. Use it properly or you will lose it.

37

Great Mystery

ORIGINAL SOURCE

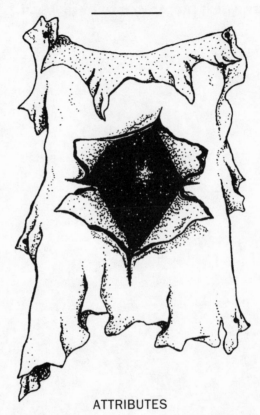

ATTRIBUTES
Source of the mysteries and all life and all love • All That Is
• The Creative Force, The Creator • The inner and outer Source •
The Divine Plan and Maker

CHALLENGES
Acknowledging the Original Source living inside of all Creation
• Not trying to solve the Mystery • Accepting the role of cocreator to the Creator •
Being a living extension of the Great Mystery's love
• Trusting the Great Mystery and the Divine Plan •

Individual Applications

If Great Mystery has spoken to you through the cards today, rejoice, for Creation is at work in your life. Be grateful for the blessings of life, breath, health, and abundance. If you should feel that one or all of these blessings is lacking in your present situation, give thanks for them as though you have received these gifts of life and they will become actively present again.

The Great Mystery card may well be telling you to drop the limitations in your personal creativity and look to the idea of being created in the image of a limitless creative Source. In recognizing the expression of Great Mystery's Creation that you represent, you may need to remind yourself that you too are a limitless cocreator of this universe. The limitations in consciousness have got to go! If you have made a mess of your present situation look at how much creativity it took to do that. All that is necessary now is for you to reverse that same flow of creativity and recreate your reality in beauty. The potential is present if you are in harmony with the universal flow; physical matter always follows thought.

Great Mystery can also be speaking to you on another level and saying that the time has come to stop trying to figure out why and how the world and your personal affairs work. The Void of the unknown is immune to your internal dialogue and your chattering fears. The future is always bright for those who trust who they are and their ability to create in the present. In feeding the positive ideas we create positive results.

Another message of the Great Mystery card has to do with your ability to honor your present path of Creation. Can you say to yourself that the role you are presently playing contributes to the whole? Do you actually feel that the talents you have are being used fully or wisely? Are you happy with the promise each new day brings? Are you willing to be here on our Earth Mother and find the joy of being physical? If you answered no to any of these questions, you have forgotten your connection to Great Mystery. You may have forgotten how precious the essence of life is to you. Do not create a crisis that will force you to remember the gift of life. Make the decision to learn and grow through creating joyful experiences instead of high drama. Then prepare yourself for the exquisite experience of feeling Great Mystery alive and well and living through you.

If you have become hopeless or helpless, it may be time to call on the omnipotent power that Great Mystery represents through words of thanksgiving for the blessings you presently have. The help you may need is living in your own heart. The atoms that make up Creation carry the spark of life Great Mystery gave them before the beginning of time. The joy is claimed when we can acknowledge that the force is alive and well inside us. All that is required is to open the heart to that Eternal Flame that lives within and is called love.

In all cases, the Great Mystery calls for a time of returning to the Original Source and acknowledging the Mystery of life. We are not asked to be detectives or to solve the Mystery but rather to bathe in the magic of discovering and rediscovering the potential for being limitless cocreators of our world and all other worlds. The magnificence of being alive and the willingness to be the source of all that we experience is a key to unlocking our potential. As we reflect the Original Source as it lives inside us, we Walk in Beauty along the Sacred Path that leads to wholeness. Even the crooked trails that cross our path from time to time are a part of the Great Mystery's plan. When we learn what is not right for us by following the crooked trail, we may then return to the Original Source and share our newfound knowing. In this manner, every part of Creation contributes to the omnipotence of the Great Mystery by giving back to the Source that which we have learned through our physical experience.

38

Field of Plenty

IDEAS/NEEDS MANIFESTED

ATTRIBUTES

Giving thanks before needs are met
• Allowing positive ideas to make space for abundance •
Visualizing the concepts of abundant living
• Manifesting those ideas in our lives through faith and positive actions •

CHALLENGES

Fearing scarcity • Lacking trust • Being greedy • Feeling undeserving
• Forgetting to give thanks • Overcoming the inability to express needs •
Imagining abundance in your life

Individual Applications

If the Field of Plenty card has come to you today, it may be time to count your blessings. It is a sure sign that you are in need of giving thanks for the abundance already in your life or for the abundance that you are asking to come to you.

Through the gratitude sent to Great Mystery, each Two-legged can tap the Field of Plenty and begin to manifest what is needed in their lives. If trust is not living in your heart, the doubt must first be cleansed. The Field of Plenty card may require that you spend some time rediscovering the faith and childlike innocence that allowed you to trust when you were younger. The skepticism and doubt that hounds many modern adults has been learned through experience. These doubts are based on past disappointments. The one element that was probably missing in those disappointing experiences was giving gratitude for the blessing *before* it actually appeared in your life. This is one way trust can be developed in hearts hardened by life's disappointments or pain. Release the old pain and be grateful you can heal that in order to make way for future abundance to enter.

The Field of Plenty reminds us that every day is Thanksgiving and that we are always asked to share our abundance with others. This reminder may apply to your life if you have been afraid to spend a dime on yourself or another person. The fear of scarcity can stop your flow of abundance. Sharing opens the Field of Plenty and allows you to receive to the degree that you are willing to give in order to move abundant energy through your life. This is not to say that you should be reckless about spending money or that you should not work and expect your lack of effort to produce miracles. The energy we spend toward balanced living is one way we open the doors for abundance to enter.

Wasting anything is a sad situation. If you have been mindless of the needs of others and have thrown away anything usable, it may be time to recycle some of the usable items you no longer need. In learning to find a use for something you are honoring its mission and giving it further purpose. This new way of perceiving the missions of all physical items can help develop new creativity within you. Senior citizen centers everywhere can often use old yarn, beads, and other items for their craft classes. You may be able to fill their needs. You have then used abundance in a proper way and have made room for more to enter your life.

The keynote of the Field of Plenty is that all we will ever need is still in thought form and is waiting to manifest. We must first be clear on what our needs are. Envision those needs and then give gratitude for the path they are following in order to manifest in your life. Trusting and eliminating doubt and then taking action by filling your life with productive creativity is the formula. Don't sit and wait. Get on with life. Filling your life with rich experience stops doubts from entering. It doesn't cost anything to take a morning walk or to watch a sunset. These experiences along with being productive show your intention to create the space for manifestation. If you don't have a job, working as a volunteer will open new doors to the Self and begin the flow of needs met.

In all cases, the Field of Plenty is asking us to look at our attitudes about trust, gratitude, giving, receiving, wasting, and hoarding. If any of your personal attitudes are blocking the natural flow of abundance in your life, change them and be joyful in doing so. In this way, Great Mystery feels your Celebration of Life and is ready to fill your needs through the Field of Plenty. Remember, the beauty of the full moon or the smile of a child are also forms of abundance. Never confuse your needs with frivolous desires that would not make you feel any more whole. You are beauty. Your sense of Self should never be weighed by what you have or who you know.

39

Stone People

RECORDS/KNOWING REVEALED

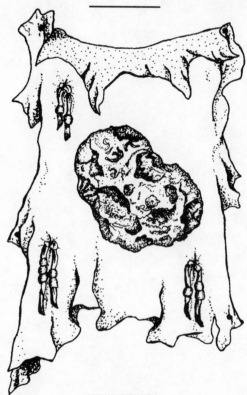

ATTRIBUTES

Finding knowledge • Accessing inner knowing and the history of Earth
• Understanding Self through Stone Teachers •
Allowing your personal history to be revealed
• Connecting to other times and spaces • Rekindling the Soul's memory •

CHALLENGES

Listening/feeling • Using intuition • Staying earthed or grounded
• Developing sensory perceptions • Trusting the truth •
Owning the ability to know • Breaking old habit patterns

Individual Applications

If a Stone Person has rolled your way today, you are being asked to reconnect with the history of Mother Earth, your personal history, your physical being, your inner knowing, and Stone Medicine. The teachings of the Stone People are available to you at this time so you might want to go out into nature and find the Teaching Stone who is calling you. Remember that this ancient friend is crossing your path for a reason. You might need to develop your intuition by turning the Stone every direction to see if any faces or animals appear on its surface. Then ask each one you find what it is telling you. The lessons will vary depending upon your present situation. At the very least, the destiny of your present Earth Walk could be revealed.

If you are trying to change or break a habit in your life, the Stone People card can be telling you to find a Rock Person who will calm you or protect you from the hustle-bustle in your life that triggers your unwanted habits or nervousness. In this case, a Stone Person may be held in your hand or worn in a small bag around your neck for easy access when your compulsion hits. It is best to use an ordinary rock rather than a crystal or mineral that conducts specific energies. The Stone Person found in a creek or along a trail is more apt to have an earthing influence on you so that you feel your Earth-connection and physical being.

Another message of the Stone People card is one of discovery. It may be time to answer some of those internal questions that have been bugging you. If you have recently found it difficult to Enter the Silence or to know your personal truth, the Stone Person may be the tool you need to quiet your internal dialogue. Try to hold the Stone in your left hand while being silent and see if this helps. If not, keep adding Stones until you feel the earthing influence and serenity of these Rock Teachers. It may take quite a few Stones if you have been doing a lot of journeying or if you have allowed the hurry disease to rule your present path.

The Stone Person is one aspect of the Earth Mother that can assist you in feeling where you belong. If you have recently felt as if you are here on Earth through some giant cosmic mistake, you have lost your Earth-connection. In losing the umbilical cord that connects you to your physicality and our Earth Mother, it is natural to feel like a fish out of water. The lie that is easiest to swallow is that any of us are here through a mistake. We are all here to learn what we can from each other and to live in harmony, finding joy in the sacredness of being physical. The Stones may be telling you that you cannot find your purpose or mission because you are floating in some dreamland full of nightmares and doubt. If this seems like it fits your present situation, ask for assistance from a Stone Person. Seek to reconnect to the nurturing of the Earth Mother and discover the pleasures of being alive. Be sure that you are willing to receive the joy that is your right as a Child of Earth. Then give yourself permission to celebrate.

The Stone People card is also asking us to seek the different forms of wisdom that Rock Medicine has to offer. We are being asked to use the gifts the Stone People offer to enrich our lives and our understanding. Every Stone on our planet is a library of gathered energy and information. If you are seeking to heal any type of wound—emotional, mental, physical, or spiritual—the Stone Tribe can give you information on how to begin that self-healing process. These Rock People are messengers for the Earth Mother and can relay her caring and devotion for all her children.

The final message of the Stone People card is that true knowing is about to be revealed. This knowledge is based in the truth that has come from this oldest of Earth Tribes, not from the opinions of others. It applies to you personally and can assist you in developing your gifts of inner knowing so that your path becomes illuminated.

40

Great Smoking Mirror

REFLECTIONS

ATTRIBUTES
Seeing other images of Self through others • Eliminating the "I"
• Instigating the "we" • Recognizing all things as one •
Learning life's lessons through observing and applying

CHALLENGES
Looking/seeing • Abolishing hierarchy • Accepting the equality of all life-forms
• Replacing self-importance by esteem for all • Seeing the reflection of truth •

Individual Applications

If Great Smoking Mirror has appeared in your spread today, you are being asked to look at Another One of Yourself who is currently in your life. Any human, Stone Person, Creature-being, Standing Person, or Cloud Person can be the other one of yourself that appears. This other reflection of you may be your exact opposite or very similar in nature. If the direct opposite appears and is very happy when you are sad, look at the joyful gift that reflection can give you. You may adjust your attitude about the present situation through the balance you have seen reflected in a joyful other-self mirror.

If you are seeking guidance or asking a question, the Smoke has to clear before you can address the real issue that is bothering you. This issue needs clarity. Perhaps it is time to address your criticizing manner. It may be that you are overly critical of yourself. If this is not the case and you have a bone to pick with someone else that is not getting resolved, look to the Self and see if you can stand in the other person's moccasins for a moment. Then look back at yourself and see just exactly what you have been making him or her feel through your actions. Is it fear, jealousy, betrayal, joy, compassion, weariness, or frustration? If you can see from the viewpoint of the other person, the situation may take on new meaning and allow you to make peace with the present challenge.

Having compassion for the situations of others, without destroying the Sacred Space of the Self, is another lesson of Great

Smoking Mirror. The needs of others can be viewed with compassion without draining energy or resources from the Self. When we give too much energy to worrying about others or parenting them so that they do not take action for themselves, we have defeated the purpose of compassion. The Smoking Mirror also shows us that if we are strong enough to make our own way in life, we can encourage others to do the same assisted by our compassion and emotional support. This is one reflection that teaches every person to care and share to the degree that makes others more able to develop the ability to do things for themselves. Equal partners make the best teams. Then the *we* is stronger than *I*.

Another message of Great Smoking Mirror is that if you have been keeping to yourself too long, it is time for other reflections. Go out and be around others who can instill you with joy. Seek new ideas and experiences; don't wait for the world to come to you. You may find that lack of new input is stilting your attitude or growth potential. New reflections found in others are gifts to the Self who yearns for adventure.

The gift of the Great Smoking Mirror is the removal of illusion that blinds us to our own self-importance. When we see the smoke clear and realize that we have been fooled into believing that some are greater or more gifted than we are, the cosmic Trickster has had the last laugh. The illusion clears and our fear of being unworthy stares back at us. Sometimes unworthiness insists we feel puffed up and grander than the next person, or that we hide our gifts. In humility we see the joke and must laugh at the self-importance that hides our unworthy shame. It will leave if we can love it with compassion and see through the illusion created by earlier pain.

In all cases, the Great Smoking Mirror calls for equality through pointing out the similarities that all life-forms may teach you. The ideas of blame, shame, and regret have no place in the present moment. Drop the smokescreen of lost or old memories and move into the clarity of present reflections which are available. When we ask, "Mirror, mirror on the wall, who's the fairest of them all?" from Great Smoking Mirror the answer comes forth through the smoke, "All reflections are equal."

41

Shaman's Death

DEATH AND REBIRTH

ATTRIBUTES
Ending and beginning • Stopping and changing gears • Harvesting and planting • Completing old cycles • Birthing new dreams, visions, and realities • Burying the past and facing the future

CHALLENGES
Regretting actions or words • Fearing death • Fearing birth • Starting over • Letting go • Fearing what tomorrow brings •

Individual Applications

If Shaman's Death has appeared today, you are being asked to notice which pattern of personal evolution you are experiencing. Are you fertilizing and preparing your life in order to meet the future? Are you planting the seeds of some new activity? Are the seeds of earlier ideas being weeded and fed so that they will continue to grow? Are you harvesting the fruits of your labors? Or are you burning off the old crop and plowing it under to make ready for new life?

Notice how each one of these cycles has a next step to the process. The continuance of growth is assured when we can visualize the next step without getting stuck where we are. This *letting go* process can take many forms. The willingness to surrender to the flow of your own creation and to trust your process can be difficult. The act of surrendering takes faith and trust. You may not feel ready for rebirth because of your attachments to what should, could, or would have been.

Regrets are formed when we do not relish the moments along the way and use to the fullest the opportunities presented to us. Plans and dreams that did not get harvested in our last cycle of growth are the forms our regrets take. Look deeply at the grief you may hold around these regrets and be willing to feel it. Then bury that old grief as a gift to the world in order to fertilize your new field of dreams with joy. The new dreams may not yet have sprouted and come to the surface of your consciousness, but they are there. Feeding these visions with new promise and nurturing their potential is the strength of your rebirth cycle.

To eliminate any further blockage to your path, ask yourself which roles you are playing in life that no longer feel alive. If you feel like a robot at work, this may be one area where your creativity has died. If your romantic interest no longer excites you, your passion may have cooled to the point that a change of some sort is necessary. This does not necessarily mean you need to destroy the relationship, but rather, use some creativity to fan the embers of a once roaring fire. If on the other hand, you have grown in a different direction from a friend or loved one, the decision to move ahead with your own personal growth might support your rebirth.

Another message of the Shaman's Death card is discernment. Look at those things within the Self that are inhibiting your growth. You might need to notice the justifications or denials that stop you from giving those shadow-parts the death penalty. The changing of old habits takes courage and conviction. When you make a decision to change any habit or personality trait, be sure that you are doing it for yourself and not because of pubic opinion or the whims of another. If your rebirth is created by another's decision, it could end in disaster. Pay attention to any inner voices that create guilt or criticism and banish those voices until you reach the joyful voice of truth in your heart.

Fear is a big contributor to blocking the idea of change. If you feel any fear about changing your life, breathe deeply until the fear subsides. Confronting and releasing the fear is one way of conquering the shadow within you. The fear that is denied and swallowed will rear its ugly head at a later date in the hope of devouring your future dreams. Don't let your life be controlled by fears that are usually based in recalling the horror stories of others. Irrational fears come from those persons who lack the courage to confront the reality they are creating. You do not need to take on the inabilities of others. Find the joy of opportunity in dealing with your own.

In all cases, Shaman's Death calls for the death of some attitude, activity, feeling, relationship, or habit that no longer serves your growth. The positive side of this death is that the ecstasy of rebirth is the next step in the process.

42

Hour of Power

RITUAL OF JOY

ATTRIBUTE

Celebrating life • Acknowledging the beauty and potential of the Self
• Seeing perfection in the moment and feeling it •
Connecting totally • Loving being alive

CHALLENGES

Not being critical • Stopping to smell the roses
• Reconnecting with the Earth Mother to be fed • Loving the Self •
Feeling the power of being human and alive at this time

Individual Applications

If you have chosen the Hour of Power card you are being asked, first, to do this ritual on a regular basis so that you can feel the joy of Earth connection. Second, focus on the beauty of this connection and know that balance feeds further exaltation. Third, realize that you can call on and re-create that feeling at any time. After you have learned these steps to self-mastery and acknowledged those abilities in the Self, you may teach others how to find that same joy.

Remember times when it seemed as if everything you touched was either very good or very bad? In both cases, you may now recall that your internal timing was either sheer perfection or sheer madness. If things are backfiring in your life presently, it is time to look at how to correct your ideas of judgment. To do so, you must slow down and find the heartbeat of the Earth Mother. Relax and align your heart with the beat of Mother Earth's inner rhythm. If you can't feel the beat, listen to some soothing music and gently move with it until you find the rhythm. Your body will begin to align with its own timing and feel the proper movement. Pay attention to your body and allow it to tell you which movements feel right. In doing this little exercise, the body's need to synchronize with the Earth's rhythm is met, and you come into oneness with your physical form as your body, mind, and spirit support your ability to feel whole.

When you sense the wholeness, your next lesson is to love that perfection, in the moment, and give it your joy. The art of loving the Self and acknowledging the abilities one has and is further developing is an act of pleasure. All acts of pleasure belong to the Earth Mother and are shared with all her children freely and abundantly. The test is to take the time to reconnect.

Further along, the lessons of the Hour of Power may take a different trail. If you feel secure in the first lessons of using the Ritual of Joy, this card may imply that it is time to learn how to funnel or transmit that joyful energy to others. Remember that this is your energy and is to be *shared but not given away,* which would leave you with emptiness. You may recycle this newfound energy through healing, prayer, assisting others in learning about their unique paths, or through any creative endeavor. The choice is always yours.

It is always proper and timely to use these same joyous energies to celebrate Earth and life. To honor All Our Relations and share life's dance is sacred. The return flow of shared bliss may be a wonderful surprise for you. All life-forms have been waiting for the Two-leggeds to wake up and receive the bliss they funnel our way, every hour of the day. Remember, all creatures have a different Hour of Power, hence, all hours are covered and none of us is ever alone. Every Tribe in the kingdoms of animals, trees, stones, clouds, wind, stars, humans, and so on shares in creating the power of joy in every hour of day or night. Together, we sustain the energy of that bliss, which comes from connection to Great Mystery, Mother Earth, and each other. Now is the time to accept the responsibility of sharing our happiness so that all Children of Earth may know this celebration of life.

In all instances, the Hour of Power calls you to recognize your role in the Divine Plan and to celebrate your path and process. Find joy in the blanket you are weaving, see the colors of the threads you hold and how they bring out the colors held by others. Tap the place within the Self that releases regret and fosters no losses. Then it is possible to know that you are the Earth Mother's child and a reflection of her joy.

43

Give-Away Ceremony

RELEASE

ATTRIBUTES
Letting Go • Giving to another without expectations • Relinquishing control
• Clearing away the past • Sharing from the heart with no strings attached •
Removing blockages to growth • Detaching from old ideas

CHALLENGES
Releasing attachment to material objects • Giving for favors later
• Destroying greed or jealousy • Letting go of fear •
Banishing need for recognition • Fearing scarcity

Individual Applications

If the Give-Away card has appeared in your spread today, you may be asked to look at your attitudes on sharing and abundance. Are you able to give a personal possession away without feeling regret? Are you hoarding items you do not use? Do you fear scarcity? Are you forgetting to trust Great Mystery's ability to manifest what you need? Is your sense of Self in need of a reality adjustment because you relate who you are to what you have or who you know?

If any of these questions applies to you, it may be time to begin your personal Give-Away. You may choose to give a few of your clothes to those in need or clean out your garage and contribute those items to charity. You may even decide to give a friend a possession of yours that he or she has always admired, so that you can feel the joy of nonattached giving. In this way, we release jealousy or greed.

On another level, it may be time to clean out your thoughts regarding your inability to create abundance in your life. Count your blessings and look at how much you have to be grateful for. Don't forget that you may receive as much nurturing from Nightingale's song as you can from an extra pair of tennis shoes. Look at the ways in which you are nurtured by your possessions and see if you can substitute a day in nature once in a while instead of a wild shopping or eating spree. There should be no guilt in having nice belongings. Notice whether you are using your possessions as a crutch to quell some uneasiness you feel about yourself. If your sense of well-being is intact, you will not be attached to your belongings out of fear of not being you without them.

On yet another level, the Give-Away card is asking you to release anything in your life that does not apply to your present state of growth. This can be the release of old habits, acquaintances who drain you, friends who no longer see life the way you do, the need for approval or recognition, old goals that no longer apply, or any aspect of your life that no longer serves you. Releasing the old will make space for new experiences, new people, and new abundance.

Remember that sacrifice originally meant *to make sacred*. In making every action and every moment in our lives sacred, we are living the eternal Give-Away. We can release the old and make way for the new by taking only what we need. In this way we assure a future of abundance for the next seven generations of humankind. When we use everything we receive to its fullest potential, we are honoring the Medicine of each thing. Everything in life has a mission of service to the rest of Creation. Using all talents and gifts to their fullest ensures abundance because nothing is wasted and the sacredness of all life-forms is honored.

In all cases, the Give-Away card teaches us how to release our attachments to who we are, what we think, habits we employ, defenses we use, addictions, compulsions, obsessions, material crutches, or identities that no longer serve us. Ridding the Self of attachments through total release is a sure pathway to personal freedom. Attachments can form any time the shadow-self feels threatened by a situation. In our need to feel loved and wanted, we oftentimes develop attachments to things that comfort our insecurity. These attachments stop the true Self from releasing the shadowy fears that gather, because instant comfort has covered the hurt. To release these attachments we are asked first to acknowledge them for what they are and give them away as our gift to the world. This act of release is the universal Give-Away that marks a major Rite of Passage. The healed healers who emerge from this Give-Away Rite of Passage can change the lives of those around them and give the world new promise.

44

Sacred Space

RESPECT

ATTRIBUTES
Commanding respect • Being respectful
• Finding Sacred Space in between the in-breath and out-breath •
Honoring the space of all living things • Cherishing the space you command
• Respecting the body and the total being •

CHALLENGES
Loving the Self • Seeing equality in the right to be for all life-forms
• Maintaining balance • Honoring every role in the universe •
Holding your Sacred Space and point of view
• Discerning who or what to allow in your Sacred Space •

Individual Applications

If the Sacred Space card has appeared in your spread today, you are being asked to respect some area of your life that has gone untended for a while. Do you need sleep? Has your appearance suffered from neglect? Do any of your possessions need repair? Have you been ignoring your personal needs in favor of the wants of others? If any of these questions apply, your self-respect is languishing.

The Sacred Space card may also be calling you in a different way. If you have not respected the ideas, belongings, homes, or bodies of other people, you are being asked to note how you would feel if they behaved that way in your Sacred Space.

Another application of this card has to do with the examination of your attitudes. Do you buy or use sprays that destroy our ozone? Do you buy or use cosmetics that use Creature-beings for testing or animal by-products as contents? Are you aware of the mistreatment of a pet in your neighborhood? Do you litter the body of our Earth Mother with refuse? Are you investing in companies that abuse the ecology or natural balance of our planet? Would you be afraid if you knew that our common Sacred Space, the Earth Mother, could no longer provide for us because of these abuses?

Look at how every action you may be involved in can assist or destroy our shared Sacred Space. See what legacy you are creating for future generations. Each one of us has a part to play in assisting our Earth Mother by simply becoming aware of the products or actions we support or refuse to buy.

Sacred Space is invaded and destroyed daily by those who refuse to see the overall picture. They may be very shocked when those actions finally hit home on personal levels. The quality of life is totally dependent on the Two-leggeds of humankind learning to love themselves enough to command respect for all life.

The Sacred Space card brings many lessons and messages; the foremost is the lesson that *all space* is Sacred Space. Look at the Creature-beings, Standing People, Creepy-crawlers, and Stone People who endure human abuse without recourse. We are not helpless. We can start by cleaning up our own backyards, our attitudes, and our actions. This is one form of learning self-respect. When we respect ourselves and all life, we then hold a point of view that allows us to command more space, use more talents, and walk in balance as guardians of the planetary Sacred Space.

Go into the silence of your favorite place in nature and walk among your relatives of the Planetary Family. Listen to them and ask what it is that they suggest for you personally. Teach children what you have learned and honor their Sacred Spaces and opinions as you would your own. They are wise people in small bodies; trust them. The children are our tomorrows and have the right to live in harmony with their happy, healthy Earth Mother. Adults are endowed with the mission of teaching through example and being the role models for the children of future generations. Through us, children learn respect for Self.

To find the center of your Sacred Space you can take a breath and briefly hold it, then exhale. Sacred Space exists in between the in-breath and the out-breath. By stopping the rhythm of a shallow or panicked breath, we can come into balance again and reclaim our Sacred Space and point of view. This remedy allows us to then respect all things as having the right to heal any imbalance. When we adopt this point of view, there is no need to be hard on ourselves during our own healing process.

In all cases, the Sacred Space card insists that we honor the role of every life-form in the universe. The ugly, the hateful, the bitter can be transformed if the right to be is honored. These mirrors of our own shadows will no longer be necessary when we tend to our own gardens and heal the reflection within our own Sacred Spaces. To cherish the total Self is to show the world how respect can heal all things, and how that healing always begins at home.

SECTION TWO

New Spreads

Since every aspect of life has many changes and questions along the way, I decided to design some spreads for those situations that need an overall view with each aspect of the bigger picture addressed. As you may remember, the new spreads were mentioned in the chapter entitled "How to Use This Workbook by Sections." I am presenting these spreads, which are designed to enhance the seeker's intuition and personal inner knowing, in order to assist each reader in developing new ways to look at various situations.

I feel that ultimately, we must come to our own conclusions and find the "yes" or "no" by asking our own hearts what is right for us. This is the reason I have not devised any spreads that will tell you what to do or how to do it. The Sacred Path Cards™ and the Medicine Cards™ are merely guidelines that enhance the seeker's own ability to see all of the pitfalls, options, and possibilities. When we have as many facts as are necessary to make our own decisions based on what we know, the action that follows becomes effortless.

The following spreads are named in honor of friends who hold special Medicine and use those abilities in their everyday lives to the fullest. These spreads teach us how to find that same Medicine within ourselves.

Morning Star Spread

The Morning Star or Dawn Star is Venus who teaches us how to greet each day and how to honor the light in our lives, which is represented by Grandfather Sun. This spread gives us the keynote of each day and shows us what our daily blessings are.

Soaring Eagle Spread

The Soaring Eagle spread teaches us to recognize our heart's desire for freedom and to be aware of the opportunities that are being presented in our lives. The Soaring Eagle sees from an expanded viewpoint and quickly snatches opportunity that leads to successful completion of the heart's desired outcome.

Pathfinder Spread

The Wolf leads the pack and finds the surest route out of the mire of confusion, fear, doubt, and uncertainty. This Pathfinder spread sheds new light on what has been confusing you and shows how to become clear and focused. The truth is found and the crooked trail ends when the Pathfinder leads you home to the true Self.

Dream Weaver Spread

In the Dream Weaver spread we are able to see below the conscious level of awareness and discover our Dreamtime wishes and visions. The object of this spread is to allow those dream images to surface so that you can face your inner desires and integrate them in your present path. This spread also shows how the dream will manifest in your life.

Vision Maker Spread

In the Vision Maker spread we are asking the cards to show us how to take the steps to making a personal vision become a reality. We learn where our limitations and challenges are in order to remove the blockages from the Sacred Path.

Morning Star Spread

The Morning Star spread sets us in motion to acknowledge the tone of each new day. We are advised of all the blessings, challenges, gifts, and lessons of each new sunrise. We are greeted by the Morning Star and Grandfather Sun and are shown how we can best approach daily activity. The layout is as follows:

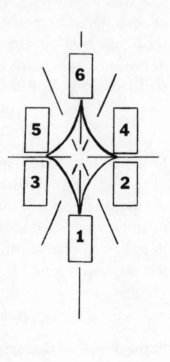

1. Card number one is the keynote lesson for the day.
2. Card number two shows the blessings we may be thankful for all day long.
3. Card number three is today's challenge.
4. Card number four is the Morning Star's gift to you.
5. Card number five is Grandfather Sun's gift to you.
6. Card number six is the gift you can share with the world today.

Soaring Eagle Spread

The Soaring Eagle spread is designed to allow our spirits to join with the essence of the Soaring Eagle in order to see with Eagle's eye all that we need to know in our quest for personal freedom. The layout is as follows:

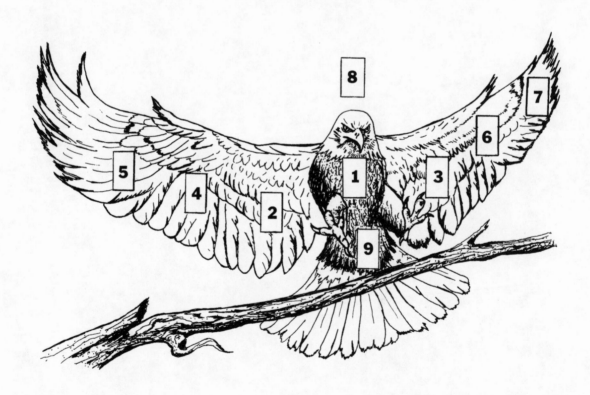

1. The first card is your lesson in the here and now.
2. The second card is your heart's desire.
3. The third card is what you need to learn.
4. The fourth card is your personal challenge.
5. The fifth card shows how to conquer that challenge.
6. The sixth card is the limitation you have created.
7. The seventh card shows how to remove the limitation.
8. The eighth card is the freedom to be gained.
9. The ninth card is the Eagle's gift to you.

Pathfinder Spread

The Pathfinder is the person who has the courage to explore possibilities and go where other less bold spirits dare not tread. The Wolf is the Medicine Guardian of those who seek out the lonely places and make the way safe for others to follow. This spread acts as the Wolf and shows us the truth in our paths as well as how to avoid the pitfalls.

1. The first card denotes where you are in your present path.
2. The second card speaks of the next safe step you can take.
3. The third card is the challenge that can make your path steep or rocky.
4. The fourth card teaches you how to avoid the pitfall of the challenge.
5. The fifth card is the Wolf's gift or teaching about this trail.
6. The sixth card is the discovery you will find at the trail's end.

Dream Weaver Spread

The Dream Weaver spread teaches us the things our dreams are made of and the Medicine that is at work in our Sleeptime Dreams. Since the subconscious is an active yet little understood partner in our reality, we need to go deeper to tap the messages our inner being is manifesting in the thought universe or Spirit World. This spread allows us to see beyond the veil of forgetting and into our heart's unspoken desire.

1. The first card represents the common thread in your dreams.
2. The second card is your heart's unspoken desire.
3. The third card reflects your hidden feelings.
4. The fourth card is your hidden talent reflected in the dream.
5. The fifth card is the dream that is emerging.
6. The sixth card is the lesson the dream is sending you.
7. The seventh card is the Dream Catcher, which will filter the negative out of your dreams and leave you with this Medicine.

Vision Maker Spread

The Vision Maker Spread is designed to allow us to see how our visions are becoming clear to the Spirit World and what challenges we have in order to make them more focused. Then the path that we must follow in order to embody our visions in the physical world is shown.

1. The first card is the Medicine the vision brings to you.
2. The second card is the lesson the vision carries.
3. The third card is the challenge to manifesting the vision.
4. The fourth card is the solution to the challenge.
5. The fifth card is the action needed to bring the vision into being.
6. The sixth card is the Medicine you need to use to assist the outcome.
7. The seventh card is the victory gift of the outcome.

Your Notes

SECTION THREE

How to Use the Cards to
Contact the Ancestors in Spirit

In this section I would like to address the intuitive use of the Sacred Path Cards™ to open the right brain and allow the messages from the Spirit World to enter. When the cards are approached in a reverent manner, they may reflect the guidance from the Spirit Realms. I have devised a spread and an exercise that will assist the seeker in tapping into his or her own power of intuition.

The Spirit World or Other Side Camp is made up of all the Totems, Ancestors, Pathfinders, Plant Spirits, Allies, and Guardians who wish to assist us in our present Earth Walks. To effectively contact these helpers, we must set aside the hurry of the modern world and Enter the Silence. In the quietness of a stilled heart and silent mind we can stop the outer world and enter the Spirit Realms. To do this we sometimes need to use tools until we are used to the shift in consciousness. The Sacred Path Cards™ can easily reflect those messages that are coming our way if we open ourselves to truly *seeing and hearing*. This type of seeing and hearing is not with the eyes and ears but rather with the heart.

When something speaks to our hearts, we know that the truth has pierced the veil of our forgetting our true Selves and a reconnection is in the works. This reconnection can be to nature, to our roots, to the true Self, to the Earth Mother and/or All Our Relations. The first step of this process is to learn to quiet the active mind and then to take it one step further by tapping our heart connection into the truth that is universal and always available. Let's begin with the Red Road/Blue Road spread.

The Red Road/Blue Road Spread

The Red Road/Blue Road spread is used for a specific purpose. If you want to find the messages and/or gifts being sent to you from the Ancestors who walk the Blue Road of Spirit, this is your tool.

The Good Red Road is the Native American term for your Earth Walk or physical life; it runs South to North on the Medicine Wheel. The Blue Road is the road of spirit where the Ancestors live in the Other Side Camp. The Ancestors are on the Blue Road to be guides and helpers to those of us who walk in the physical realm. The Blue Road is sometimes called the Black Road by the Plains Tribes and runs East to West on the Medicine Wheel.

To execute this spread in the proper manner you must assume the attitude of entering Sacred Space and allow yourself to be silent. From your heart you must send forth your permission to the Grandfathers and Grandmothers so that they may aid you in feeling, hearing, or seeing them. Without your permission, they are unable to assist. You give them permission to speak to you through the cards by asking for assistance.

Shuffle the cards and spread them in the shape of a fan in front of you so that you may feel each one and allow your fingers to be your eyes. One by one, allow your hand to be led to the proper card. Then place each card face down in its proper position. When you have completed the full layout of this spread, turn over one card at a time and read the message along with the significance of that card's position.

The power of this spread is the wisdom that can be transmitted with love by those who have gone before us. You may feel the presence of the Ancestors or hear the name of your helper/guide. Know that because you have assumed an attitude of reverence and respect, you are protected by those on the Blue Road of Spirit. If you feel fearful about trying this spread, *do not do it*. There is no need to feed any internal fears about spirits. This is a form of *high magic* and is not to be taken lightly. You may not be ready for this type of initiation and that is nothing to be ashamed about. Your time to try this spread will come when your understanding is greater, and that time will be perfect when it happens for you. Each person has their own Sacred Space and their own internal timing for experiencing life. It is your responsibility to honor what is proper and timely for you.

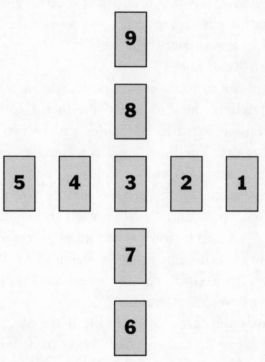

1. The first card is where you are in present time and what lesson you are working on in daily life.
2. The second card is the next lesson you will be experiencing in the near future.
3. The third card is the place where the Red and Blue Roads meet and is your present connection to both worlds. For example, this card is the tool that can put you in the proper frame of mind or state of awareness to integrate the information you are receiving.

4. The fourth card is the challenge you are now facing.
5. The fifth card is the inner wisdom you need to acknowledge in yourself.
6. The sixth card begins the Blue Road and expresses the spiritual illumination being offered by the Ancestors.
7. The seventh card is representing the limitation you may need to let go of to fulfill your present desired goals. In other words, the lesson of this card is not being applied properly and you may need to let go of an old habit pattern so that you may expand into your new state of being and awareness.
8. The eighth card is symbolizing the balance point. This balance point is an ability, a talent, a Medicine, or a gift that the Ancestors are willing to pass to you if you desire to learn the lesson of this card.
9. The ninth card is the final card of the Blue Road. This card represents union or at-one-ment with the Grandmother or Grandfather that is assisting you on your journey. In this position, this card can be the secret clue to the helper/guide's Medicine and can also be the very tool that will allow you to tap into that Ancestor's energy field. In using this last tool you may find that the union, heart to heart, is felt. Never limit the possibilities of encountering your Blue Road counterparts; you may ask for the Ancestor's name at this time and feel the presence of the loving Medicine being sent to you.

You may chose to go further and ask the Ancestor who has contacted you how she or he can help you better understand your present lessons. The choice to develop this relationship is up to you. The Ancestor may be an Ancestor of Native American origin or one who is of your own family tree. The Ancestor could be from another culture or could be your own grandmother who is in spirit. For each individual the experience will differ, and from time to time other Ancestors may choose to come forth in order to assist you on your path.

Exercise to Connect to the Spirit World

To open our intuitive abilities and to understand those Medicine Helpers who are assisting our journeys we need to access the right brain. I have devised this exercise to allow each seeker another tool that can help accomplish this task.

This exercise is designed to allow anyone seeking an answer to fully access the right or intuitive brain in order to bridge the gap between the card's meanings and the actual words that come from the Ancestors in spirit. The cards can speak to us in many ways, but when coupled with actual communication from the Spirit World, the results can be life changing.

In using the left hand to write answers we are accessing the right brain. This applies to those who are normally left-handed as well. Those people just use their right hand in order to access a different brain balance. The access to our intuitive talents can further enhance our abilities to see deeper meanings in the cards, see different combinations of cards, and discern how those grouped meanings directly apply to our lives.

First it is necessary to understand that in doing this exercise we must maintain silence and give the Allies and Ancestors permission to communicate with us by asking for assistance. Then we must tell the active mind not to interfere with our connection. We write the following questions one at a time with the right hand. Then we pick up the pen with the left hand and allow the answer to the question we just posed to be written as we feel it. If the answer you receive seems like it does not make sense to you, don't stop or judge it. Keep on and use your intuition.

Write this question with your right hand:
Who are you and why have you come to assist me?

_____

_____

Now write the answer with your opposite hand.

_____

_____

_____

_____

_____

_____

_____

Write this question with your right hand:
What can you tell me about my present situation?

_____

_____

Write the answer with the opposite hand.

_____

_____

_____

_____

_____

_____

_____

You will ask another question in the same manner and then pick a Sacred Path Card™ to give further clarity to your answer. With your right hand, write:

Which step of initiation in the cards will bring further understanding to this situation?

_____

_____

_____

Pick a card and allow this Spirit Helper to tell you why this card will assist you in the present. Write the card name here:

_____

Writing with your right hand, ask for insight by forming a question to your Spirit Helper about how the card applies to you.

_____

_____

_____

Then, using the left hand for the answer, allow the Spirit Helper to give you insight on this card's lesson.

_____

_____

_____

_____

_____

_____

_____

_____

_____

_____

_____

You may wish to pick another Sacred Path Card™ that will represent the Medicine the Spirit Helper can offer you at this time. Write the card name here:

_____

Ask your Spirit Helper how this Medicine will strengthen you on your present path and write the question below using your right hand.

_____

_____

Then allow the Spirit Helper to answer you by switching hands again and writing the answer on the following lines.

_____

_____

_____

_____

_____

_____

_____

_____

_____

_____

Following the same switching of hands method, write these next questions and allow the answers to come forward.

Where should I go in nature to reconnect with my Allies during this time?

_____

_____

Answer:_____

_____

_____

_____

What sign from you should I look for when I am there?

_____

Answer:_____

_____

_____

_____

_____

_____

Since you are helping me on my path, what can I do to help myself and others at this time?

_____

_____

Answer:_____

_____

_____

_____

_____

_____

_____

_____

Have you told me all that you wish to at this time?

_____

Answer:_____

_____

_____

_____

_____

Now that you have completed your discussion with your Spirit Helper, thanks is in order. Show your gratitude with your heart and then you may wish to pick the third card, which symbolizes the essence of the connection you have just made with the Spirit World. Write the card name here:

_____

How you feel this card applies to your experience can then be recorded below:

_____

_____

_____

_____

_____

_____

_____

_____

_____

_____

Please note that you may do this exercise many times. Anytime you feel the need or feel disconnected from those who would give you assistance, this exercise is in order.

SECTION FOUR

Using the Totems with the Sacred Path Cards™

Many of the letters I receive are from those of you who have used the Medicine Cards™, which teach us how to get in touch with aspects of our human nature through the lessons presented by our Totems or Creature-teachers. The Medicine Cards™ show us how our human behavior is also found in the characteristics of the Power Animals and how we can predict what is coming our way through those Creatures. The Sacred Path Cards™ is a set of Sacred Teachings that represent our steps along the Path of Beauty. The Path deck teaches us how to view those steps as we change and grow. When we combine the two decks we get a double meaning on every situation as well as a combined teaching that will enhance our understanding at a deeper level.

Since the Medicine Cards™ are a deck of Totem Animals, I am going to refer to them as the Totem deck in this text. The Sacred Path Cards™ are initiation steps and will be called the Path cards.

The Totem deck adds a new potential to the Path cards when they are used in tandem. In the Totem deck there are nine Blank Shield cards. None of these cards were to be added to the deck unless they were made into personal Totems for the owner of the deck, with pictures of specific animals that were not included in the original deck. Because these extra Totems are specifically connected to the individual owner of the deck, they probably do not apply when reading for another person.

I had the need to experiment further, so I have now formulated a new way to use one of the Blank Shield cards. To do this, I have added one Blank Shield card to my Totem deck in order to represent *the Void* or *unlimited potential.*

In using this blank as unlimited potential, we are also being given a key to our own creative abilities. We cannot, in this present time, possibly know all that we can be, do, have, or experience, or we would have come to the end of our Sacred Path. The Blank Shield signals a time of explosive potential if we are willing to grab the opportunities sent our way.

We could call this a *potential miracle* card or a message from the Void saying we are about to meet our potential destiny. It is a time for creativity to take hold in the present and physically change our present path.

Using indicators or second cards to clarify the cards we originally picked is the first step of going deeper into the meaning of any spread. Let's look at one example.

Path card	Totem card
North Shield	Turtle
Wisdom/Gratitude	Mother Earth/Receptive Female Energy

In reading these two cards together, we see that the seeker can find new wisdom by connecting to the Earth, the feminine side of his or her nature, by giving gratitude for the blessings he or she receives in the physical and/or honoring Mother Earth's and his or her own needs.

To gain further understanding we pick another card from the Totem deck and place it on the North Shield card and a Path card and place it on the Turtle card.

Totem card	Path card
Squirrel	Hour of Power
Gathering/Planning Ahead	Ritual of Joy/Celebration of Life

Squirrel tells the seeker that to continue receiving the wisdom of the Earth Mother and his or her own receptive nature, it is necessary to gather those gifts of wisdom and use them to plan for the future. The Hour of Power tells the seeker that the celebration of life and all rituals of joy are found through correctly applying the gathered wisdom to life plans. Because the Hour of Power is one hour during the day when each being is fed by Mother Earth's energy, another meaning can emerge. Giving gratitude through dance, celebration, joy, or ceremony allows the seeker to receive further wisdom, gather more healing energy, develop further the connection to the Earth Mother, and wisely use the new abilities.

If we chose another Totem card to give us the overall message of this set of four cards' lessons, and we pulled the Blank Shield, we would know the seeker could achieve unlimited potential or a major breakthrough by mastering these lessons.

Let's look at how we could use this new understanding of using both decks to enhance the Tipi spread.

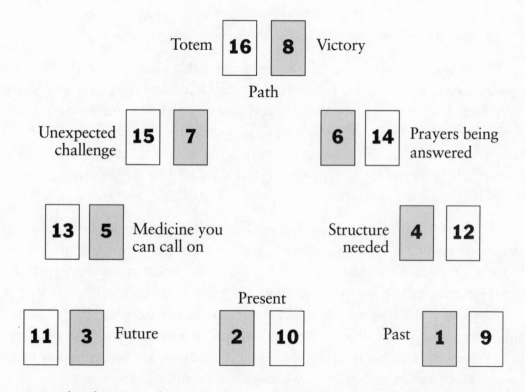

In the diagram above, cards numbered one through eight are the Path cards and cards nine through sixteen are the Totem cards. The Totems are the indicators, and they expand the meanings of the Path cards. It is best to pull all cards and leave them face down. Then each can be turned over one at a time, allowing more focus. The first card would be turned over and its meaning read from the *Sacred Path Cards™* book. Then the meaning of the Totem accompanying it would be read from the *Medicine Cards™* book. So the first and ninth cards, the second and tenth cards, and so on, are read together all the way through the spread.

1. In the Past position, I came up with Whirling Rainbow—Unity/ Wholeness Achieved. This tells me that the seeker has just finished a lesson in life and has achieved a sense of completion or unity with others or the Self, along with a new sense of wholeness. Then I turned over the Totem for an indicator and came up with Frog. Since Frog represents cleansing and then replenishment, it tells me that the seeker has successfully cleansed the old sense of identity and has replenished the Self with the new sense of unity.

2. The second card is Moon Lodge, and this tells me that the seeker is now ready to take a well-earned break. It might be time to retreat in order to mull over the completed lesson or to rest and enjoy the outcome of a job well done. The indicator is Dog, which tells me that the seeker was faithful to his or her dreams and that this Medicine assisted the successful completion. In this position, Dog can also be a reminder to be faithful to the Self and personal needs. This would follow the understanding of needing a retreat.

3. In the future position I drew the Dreamtime card which speaks of unlimited vision. In this case, the seeker is being asked to drop all limiting thoughts in order to accomplish the next step. The seeker is also being asked to use the retreat of the present to explore the other worlds in order to integrate the wholeness of unlimited unity found in the first set of cards. The indicator is Spider, which tells me that writing down the achievements of the wholeness achieved would creatively allow the seeker to expand his or her vision of the future. Since Spider is creativity, we also find promise in these future cards of creativity matched with unlimited vision, which speaks of this seeker's bright future potential.

4. The structure-needed card, in the fourth position, is Sweat Lodge, which tells the seeker that further purification is needed. The indicator tells us

what needs to be purified. This card is Grouse. Grouse is the sacred spiral of evolution, sparkling synchronicity, and unified movement. This tells the seeker that he or she should continue to remove all blockages to forward movement. These blocks could take form in hesitation, insecurity, confusion, lack of goals, or any other missed step that would stop the seeker from knowing when to leap into action.

5. In the fifth position, we have the Medicine we can call on to find the strength to meet those challenges presented in the spread. Shaman's Death appeared in this position and tells the seeker that he or she might want to use the present retreat to let go of the past lesson. This card also speaks of a time of rebirth, which will allow the seeker to integrate into his or her life a new sense of wholeness. Mouse appeared as the indicator, telling the seeker to pay attention to old patterns trying to re-emerge. Scrutiny of what belongs to the old is the keynote, as well as Mouse's warning not to feel overwhelmed by old feelings or ideas, if in fact those patterns are continuing to emerge as they release. We oftentimes fear that the patterns that are releasing on a physical cellular level are being recreated by returning to haunt us as future lessons. All that is necessary in this instance is Mouse Medicine. Thank these habit or life patterns for leaving and observe them as they go. By not being overwhelmed, we allow the old images of Self to leave of their own accord and merely note the exodus with satisfaction.

6. The South Shield appeared in the sixth position, which is the prayers being answered position in this spread. In this seeker's spread, the significance of Innocence/Inner Child is very timely. The childlike wonder, which is knowing the magic of life, is returning as a part of this seeker's rebirth cycle. The little child who still lives inside of every person is ready to assist us with reclaiming the magic of faith and innocence. It is also timely that the Raven showed as the Totem indicator. The magic is returning to the seeker's sense of Self. This position is always a place where we should give back to Great Mystery a prayer of gratitude for the unexpected gift of answers to these prayers to aid our process.

7. In the seventh position, we find our unexpected challenge. The Medicine Bundle appeared and spoke of Allies/Support. This tells me that the

seeker may not feel the presence of his or her Medicine Helpers, or that he or she may be diminishing the value of their assistance. Since this position is an unexpected challenge, it might also portend a time when the seeker is unable to reach out and ask for support from others. The clarity comes from pulling the indicator, which is Ant. The new light shed tells me that the seeker is impatient with others or him- or herself. The seeker may expect the help to have arrived yesterday, which could reflect on the Grouse in the fourth position. It would seem that another aspect of the seeker's nature in need of purification may be the sense of universal or divine timing. He or she may be trying to push the river and in that same moment, push others beyond their own natural sense of order.

8. In the victory position, we find the Painted Face card. The keynote is Self-expression. The indicator is Hummingbird—Joy/Unconditional Love. This tells me that the seeker will find the new Self and will be able to express his or her new abilities with joy when the lessons of the challenges presented by the other cards are completed. In review, this seeker must let go of conditions he or she places on those who would assist him or her. The seeker needs to continue to purify the sense of universal timing and possibly that desire to push the river for him- or herself and others. These are the seeker's personal blocks to receiving unlimited vision and creative energy flows. Victory is clear if the seeker takes the time, in the present, to retreat and reflect on the loyalty he or she owes to the new sense of wholeness and understanding of unity within the Self and the universe as a whole. The joy of self-expression tempered with unconditional love is the seeker's if he or she honors the magic of the child within and allows the death of the overwhelmed adult-self to be reborn as the innocent child who uses personal magic through self-expression.

As you can see, each card feeds the next and all sets of Path and Totem cards interrelate with the other sets. If you are applying the spread to yourself, it may be easier for you to see how it applies to your present situation. You may now use the Tipi spread with Totem indicators and see how you can relate each set of cards to their positions in the spread and then to every other card. The space below is for you to write your results.

_____

_____

_____

_____

_____

Now that you have written your results, you may choose to ask yourself the following questions:

What does the present position (number 2) tell me about the direct path to the victory card (number 8)? Am I clear about achieving that victory? Do I want to invest time in working toward that goal?

Did I notice that the unexpected challenge (position 7) has a Medicine (position 5) that will help me unravel the challenge itself?

How do the unspoken prayers being answered in my life apply to my present situation (position 6)?

How can I apply the structure I need (position 4) to my life in order to achieve the victory (position 8)?

Use the space below to write your answers.

_____

_____

_____

_____

_____

_____

_____

_____

_____

_____

_____

_____

_____

_____

_____

After you have formulated some of your own answers you may wish to do the Tipi spread with Totem indicators for a few friends in order to gain further insight.

The next step will be learning how to understand contrary Totems as indicators without placing them in a spread, but rather by looking at two cards (one from each deck) and discerning the many double meanings possible with contrary indicators.

Anytime you get a contrary Totem as an indicator you are being asked to look at both sides of the Totem's lesson and to ask yourself which one applies to the situation. If you are reading for someone else, you should _never_ assume that the seeker is out of balance. A true teacher asks if the seeker if has felt the influence of the contrary lesson. For instance, in the Tipi spread that we looked at where Ant was the indicator with the Medicine Bundle, the Ant was not contrary. And yet, because this was the unexpected challenges position, I framed a few possible questions for the seeker. Ant is patience. I took the contrary meaning as impatience and applied it to help from others, assistance from the Allies, the seeker's impatience, and the other cards. The seeker would then have to decide how it applied to him or her.

Let's look at a few examples:

Sacred Space (Respect) with Crow (Law)

Since Sacred Space teaches us how to command respect from others and how to respect ourselves and the Sacred Space of all other life-forms, we may then look at the indicator of Crow, which is Divine Law, not the laws of humankind. (See page 133 in the *Medicine Cards™* book.) Divine Law gives all life-forms irrevocable rights. We can only destroy those rights by giving them away or by not honoring them. In the Medicine story about Crow, he pecked at his shadow until it woke up and ate him. That is to say that if we pick, pick, pick at what is wrong with us instead of focusing on what is right with us, we give validity to our own shadowy nature, and it can devour us. This is the truth of contrary Crow. The Great Mystery sees our essence and potential and allows us to feed our shadows or to nurture the true Self through our free will. The lack of respect in this case could be caused by the seeker's critical Crow voice picking at his or her own shadow to wake it up and destroy his or her own Sacred Space. This same trait could be used against others through the seeker's being critical of them, thus inflicting harm on their Sacred Space.

Pipe (Prayer/Inner Peace) with Opossum (Strategy)

The inner peace that allows us to approach life in a prayerful or reverent manner is embodied in the Pipe, which balances the male and female within us. In its most simple form, contrary Opossum is lack of strategy. When a person does not have a plan, there is confusion, doubt, fear, and usually a lack of commitment present. In this combination of Opossum and Pipe, prayers cannot be answered because of a lack of knowing what one's needs are. Inner peace cannot be found because there is no plan or strategy on how to reach that place within the Self.

Coral (Nurturing) with Rabbit (Fear)

The Coral card speaks to us of the Planetary Family, all of the Earth Mother's children, and how all are loved equally and are striving to love and nurture one another as well. How we nurture others and how we nurture ourselves may be opposing actions. If we feel that others need more than we do, we may be nurturing our own sense of unworthiness. If we feel we need more nurturing than others, we may be nurturing a victim role within us. If we give to others and do not allow them to give back to us, we may be afraid of receiving. When Coral shows with the Rabbit card in the contrary, we see that the seeker may be paralyzed by a fear of relationships of all kinds. A lack of connection to any healthy nurturance could have been present in this seeker's life. This could signal a total emotional shutdown or a refusal to interact with anyone who could nurture the seeker. If, on the other hand, this fear could be handled by the seeker's beginning to interact with others who can nurture him or her in a healthy manner, the seeker could create new relationships, receive nurturing, and nurture others again.

Thunder-beings (Usable Energy) with Otter (Woman Medicine)

The Thunder-beings card speaks of energy being funded to the seeker at a time when it may be used in a way that will enhance growth. The Thunderers live in the West of the Medicine Wheel and, therefore, are the forerunners of future events. To receive contrary Otter with the Thunder-beings card, the seeker is put on notice that, unlike Otter who moves every two days, the seeker seems stuck in the same old rut. The other meaning of Otter, which is balanced Woman Medicine, has become imbalanced. Otter, the coquette (which in French means innocent, playful child and is applied to both genders), is playful and joyous in moving with and using energy. The seeker may, in this instance, take a look at which part of his or her movement has become stilted due to self-imposed limitations. The keynote here is that energy is being supplied and stopped by the seeker. To remove the blockage, the seeker may choose to get some exercise, remove limiting ideas, not take life so seriously, or simply balance the female side of his or her nature in order to receive the energy being funded. On another level, the Thunder-beings are a male energy, and with contrary Otter, the significance could be that the male side of the seeker's nature is overpowering the feminine aspect. Too much exposure and not enough quiet time could be the imbalance.

It is now time for you to pick three Path cards and three contrary Totems. Make notes as to your interpretations and your results in the space provided below.

_____

_____

_____

_____

_____

_____

_____

_____

_____

_____

_____

_____

_____

_____

_____

Finally, you may now want see how you perceive the contrary cards. Do you see them as bad? Do you understand that they are a tool to use in discovering your limitations as well as in learning how to conquer those blockages? Can you understand why there is no bad Medicine in the cards? The contrary cards merely suggest that there are lessons and areas of life where we can continue to improve our understanding of our human and animal natures. In so doing, we are able to free the limitless, creative spirits within us and fly.

SECTION FIVE

Using Both Decks to Find
Your Path of Beauty

Every one of the Sacred Path Cards™ brings a new level of understanding or set of lessons. In a sense, each card represents a new level of initiation, which will help the seeker to clarify which path to follow, how to get there, what to look for along the way, and how to master the lessons involved. To help you further understand how to get to the deeper meaning each card offers, there are a few tools I would like to share.

If a card's meaning is not clear to you, pick a Totem card and place it next to the Path card to tell you how it applies. For example, if you pick the Sun Dance card, you may not be clear on what limitation you need to sacrifice in your life. If you then drew the Badger card you would be clear that in the situation in question, you were being too aggressive. It would then be time to sacrifice any aggression toward others and to aggressively heal yourself.

In another instance, you may have picked the Moon Lodge card, which tells you that you need time alone or a retreat from some activity. To gain further clarity, you might pick the Deer card, which tells you that you need to be gentle with the Self. The Moon Lodge card with the Mountain Lion card would be telling you that you must take the lead in demanding time for yourself or time to decide what the next leadership move would be or time to reflect on how to lead through example.

Every combination gives new and deeper meaning to the next growth pattern you are entering and achieving. I have devised a way for each person to look at the three steps they are dealing with in their present lesson. The following diagram makes it easy to understand.

The Beauty Way Spread

Path Card 5 Future Completion	Path Card 3 Next Step	Path Card 1 Lesson Already Begun
Medicine Card 6 Indicator of area applied	Medicine Card 4 Indicator of area applied	Medicine Card 2 Indicator of area applied

The Beauty Way spread is an overall view of our chosen path of lessons to be learned in life. We view past present and future in order to see where we have been, where we are now, and where we are going. These are exemplified by the Sacred Path Cards™. How those lessons will appear to us and/or how we will relate to the lessons as they apply to different areas of our lives is indicated by the Totems.

In using the Beauty Way spread, you are given a reality of where you stand in any given situation. Let us say that the first Path card was Peyote Ceremony. This would tell us that the seeker had begun to develop a new skill in some area of life. The second card might be the Rabbit. This would tell us that the new skill could be overcoming fear. Since Rabbit's other gifts are listening, fertility, and warning us not to become paralyzed, the indication could also point to the new ability being found through listening. It might also indicate that learning or using this new talent was shadowed by the person's fear or doubt. Now you may also derive your own possible meanings by viewing both cards and their significance. In so doing, you further develop your intuitive abilities.

Let us say that card number 3 was the Stone People card. Since this card represents Earth Records and Knowing Revealed, it would be safe to say that the present has brought some new understanding. This could come from connecting to nature using crystals or stones, finding past-life recall, or feeling a connection to some part of history you came upon. Since the first set of cards revealed a new ability being developed, the second card adds meaning to the new skill by saying that a breakthrough is in progress.

Card 4 could have been the Ant card, which implies that patience is necessary to complete the full understanding of how to use the new talent. Since all of the contrary Totem messages apply, the warning is not to be impatient with one's learning process.

The fifth card can be the Counting Coup card, which expresses victory over the challenges presented through learning to use the new talent or ability. The sixth card turned up as the Hummingbird, which speaks of the joy attained by persevering through the steps of the lessons along the Beauty Way.

Now it is your turn to work. Six cards and their meanings are listed below, and you can interpret them in your own way. As you look at all of the significances, you may first want to pretend that the cards are telling you a story about someone else. This is a good way to begin the intuitive process. For instance, if the first two cards were Pow Wow and Beaver, the story might tell you that the person in question was sharing ideas and interacting with others. The purpose of this interaction would be in preparation for a quickening. The quickening is the time before giving birth, which would indicate that the seeker was about to birth a new project, level of understanding, relationship, career, or period of growth. Then the Beaver comes to tell you that the birth is related to a dream or idea the seeker is now ready to bring into physical manifestation; if you pretend the story is giving you clues so that you can fill in the blanks, it will be easy to interpret. It works best when you are actually looking at the cards listed here.

Future Completion, 5	Next Step, 3	Lesson Already Begun, 1
Council Fire	South Shield	Burden Basket
Decisions	Innocence/Inner Child	Self-reliance
Indicator, 6	Indicator, 4	Indicator, 2
Skunk	Raven	Bear
Reputation	Magic	Strength
Attract/Repel	Insight/Future	Goals/Personal Answers

Write your interpretations in the space provided below.

_____

_____

_____

_____

_____

_____

_____

_____

_____

_____

Now that you have completed the story that these six cards have told you, and you feel confident in understanding it, pick six cards for yourself from your two decks. Write down the story and how it applies to some present situation in your life. The Beauty Way spread is a deeper way to understand a daily lesson and can be expanded by picking one card from each deck and using only those two cards as the focus for your day.

Your Spread Layout

Write your interpretation of your Beauty Way spread below.

_____

_____

_____

_____

_____

After you have completed your first Beauty Way Spread you will be able to work with it in another manner. If any two cards, Path and Totem, in combination do not make sense to you, ask the cards what needs further clarity and pick a second indicator card from the Totem deck. Let's look at a couple of examples.

Sun Dance (Self-sacrifice) with Dolphin (Manna)

This could be a difficult combination. Are the cards asking you to sacrifice life-force or manna? No, of course not. But are you doing it unconsciously? I would ask the person getting the reading if he or she needed to sacrifice a self-imposed limitation on how much life-force he or she is willing to receive. I would ask the seeker to pick another indicator from the Totem deck for clarity. The card picked was Eagle. This indicates to me that the limitation has to do with personal freedom and the need to free the seeker from only receiving a tiny bit of the life-force that is available to him or her.

If the second indicator had been Lynx, I would say the limitation needing to be sacrificed was not speaking up about what the seeker needed in the form of life support or Manna. In the contrary, Lynx might be saying that the seeker was wasting life-force by talking too much rather than taking action.

In another situation, if the second indicator had been Frog, the seeker might need to cleanse old patterns by sacrificing them and filling up the Self with new Manna or life-force.

As you can see, each set of combinations tells a deeper and more intricate story. In using these techniques of picking indicators, every spread can bring you new levels of further understanding. Now you may pick three second indicator cards for your Beauty Way spread and interpret how they add deeper meaning to the story you have already begun. Then write your perceptions and interpretations below.

_____

_____

_____

_____

_____

_____

_____

_____

_____

_____

_____

_____

_____

_____

_____

_____

_____

SECTION SIX

Asking Specific Questions

It may be advantageous from time to time to ask specific questions of the Self that only the heart can answer. This can be a process of self-examination or confrontation or merely serve as a reality check. In this way we can devise a manner in which the balance of understanding can be found.

The following are some questions I have used to assist my own self-discovery process. I have asked these questions of the cards and used the Tipi spread to give myself an overall view of my personal growth process.

What lessons should I focus on in order to best enhance my growth?

What are the issues surrounding the challenge I am facing?

If I continue on my present path, what should I know about the lessons that will be a part of that path?

If I choose to alter my path and follow ___(fill in your optional path)___, what will my lessons and challenges be?

In a partnership or relationship with ___(person's name)___, what lessons and challenges can I expect to meet along that way?

How can I best use the opportunity being presented?

Which lessons and challenges are being held in my subconscious that would assist my growth?

Which lessons do the Allies of nature want to present in order to assist my growth process?

Which lessons would assist me in connecting to the Earth Mother?

Which lessons do I need to focus on in order to bring my dreams into manifestation?

Which messages or life signals are being overlooked by me in this time of confusion?

Which set of truths should I see in order to enhance my clarity in this situation?

Which lesson should I pay attention to at this time of personal transformation?

Which lessons will assist me in better accessing my personal gifts and abilities?

Which card applications will best assist me in meeting my goals?

Which teachings will allow me to find my own answers and know my own truth?

How may I better understand the viewpoint of ___(person's name)___?

On what should my focus be as I begin this new cycle in my life?

These and many other questions will allow you to see the Tipi spread from a slightly different perspective, and the answers you find may assist you in seeing new angles of the same situation. In so doing, you are then able to feel more secure in yourself and your perceptions.

Daily Progress Sheet

Date: _____   Spread Name:_____

Question or Situation: _____

_____

_____

_____

Layout and Card Positions

How did the cards speak to you through this spread? You may choose to ask yourself these questions.

What did I learn and can I now apply it to my life?

How does this information make the situation easier to handle?

What progress have I made since the last time I consulted the cards?

Have any decisions I have made affected my progress?

Have I created any limitations or hesitations in my personal path?

Has this information brought up new questions or areas I need to look at in order to further my growth?

Notes:_____

_____

_____

_____

_____

_____

_____

_____

_____

_____

_____

_____

_____

_____

_____

_____

_____

_____

_____

_____

_____

Weekly Progress Sheet

Lesson of the week: Pick one card for the overview or focus of the week you are entering or finishing. Write the name of the card here: _____

    Now add that card back into the deck and shuffle the cards before doing a spread of your choice, which will further explain the overview lesson.

Layout and Card Positions

    Write your interpretation here and note how these insights may assist your further growth.

_____

_____

_____

_____

_____

_____

_____

_____

_____

_____

_____

_____

_____

_____

_____

_____

_____

_____

_____

_____

_____

_____

_____

Now it might be good to review your earlier progress sheets to see how you are progressing. Are there similar lessons being presented week to week or are you moving quickly through the growth process? If you feel that some of your present lessons are becoming stuck patterns, you might pick one card that expresses the lesson that will assist the energy in flowing again or that will give you a tool with which to meet the challenge being presented.

Daily Progress Sheet

Date: _____   Spread Name:_____

Question or Situation: _____

_____

_____

_____

Layout and Card Positions

How did the cards speak to you through this spread? You may choose to ask yourself these questions.

What did I learn and can I now apply it to my life?

How does this information make the situation easier to handle?

What progress have I made since the last time I consulted the cards?

Have any decisions I have made affected my progress?

Have I created any limitations or hesitations in my personal path?

Has this information brought up new questions or areas I need to look at in order to further my growth?

Notes:_____

_____

_____

_____

_____

_____

_____

_____

_____

_____

_____

_____

_____

_____

_____

_____

_____

_____

_____

Weekly Progress Sheet

Lesson of the week: Pick one card for the overview or focus of the week you are entering or finishing. Write the name of the card here: _____

    Now add that card back into the deck and shuffle the cards before doing a spread of your choice, which will further explain the overview lesson.

Layout and Card Positions

    Write your interpretation here and note how these insights may assist your further growth.

_____

_____

_____

_____

_____

_____

_____

_____

_____

_____

_____

_____

_____

_____

_____

_____

_____

_____

_____

_____

_____

_____

_____

_____

_____

Now it might be good to review your earlier progress sheets to see how you are progressing. Are there similar lessons being presented week to week or are you moving quickly through the growth process? If you feel that some of your present lessons are becoming stuck patterns, you might pick one card that expresses the lesson that will assist the energy in flowing again or that will give you a tool with which to meet the challenge being presented.

Daily Progress Sheet

Date: _____   Spread Name: _____

Question or Situation: _____

_____

_____

_____

Layout and Card Positions

How did the cards speak to you through this spread? You may choose to ask yourself these questions.

What did I learn and can I now apply it to my life?

How does this information make the situation easier to handle?

What progress have I made since the last time I consulted the cards?

Have any decisions I have made affected my progress?

Have I created any limitations or hesitations in my personal path?

Has this information brought up new questions or areas I need to look at in order to further my growth?

Notes:_____

_____

_____

_____

_____

_____

_____

_____

_____

_____

_____

_____

_____

_____

_____

_____

_____

_____

Weekly Progress Sheet

Lesson of the week: Pick one card for the overview or focus of the week you are entering or finishing. Write the name of the card here: _____

Now add that card back into the deck and shuffle the cards before doing a spread of your choice, which will further explain the overview lesson.

Layout and Card Positions

Write your interpretation here and note how these insights may assist your further growth.

_____

_____

_____

_____

_____

_____

_____

_____

_____

_____

_____

_____

_____

_____

_____

_____

_____

_____

_____

_____

_____

_____

Now it might be good to review your earlier progress sheets to see how you are progressing. Are there similar lessons being presented week to week or are you moving quickly through the growth process? If you feel that some of your present lessons are becoming stuck patterns, you might pick one card that expresses the lesson that will assist the energy in flowing again or that will give you a tool with which to meet the challenge being presented.

Daily Progress Sheet

Date: _____   Spread Name:_____

Question or Situation: _____

_____

_____

_____

Layout and Card Positions

How did the cards speak to you through this spread? You may choose to ask yourself these questions.

What did I learn and can I now apply it to my life?

How does this information make the situation easier to handle?

What progress have I made since the last time I consulted the cards?

Have any decisions I have made affected my progress?

Have I created any limitations or hesitations in my personal path?

Has this information brought up new questions or areas I need to look at in order to further my growth?

Notes:_____

_____

_____

_____

_____

_____

_____

_____

_____

_____

_____

_____

_____

_____

_____

_____

_____

_____

_____

_____

Weekly Progress Sheet

Lesson of the week: Pick one card for the overview or focus of the week you are entering or finishing. Write the name of the card here: _____

    Now add that card back into the deck and shuffle the cards before doing a spread of your choice, which will further explain the overview lesson.

Layout and Card Positions

    Write your interpretation here and note how these insights may assist your further growth.

_____

_____

_____

_____

_____

_____

_____

_____

_____

_____

_____

_____

_____

_____

_____

_____

_____

_____

_____

_____

_____

_____

Now it might be good to review your earlier progress sheets to see how you are progressing. Are there similar lessons being presented week to week or are you moving quickly through the growth process? If you feel that some of your present lessons are becoming stuck patterns, you might pick one card that expresses the lesson that will assist the energy in flowing again or that will give you a tool with which to meet the challenge being presented.

Daily Progress Sheet

Date: _____   Spread Name:_____

Question or Situation: _____

_____

_____

_____

Layout and Card Positions

How did the cards speak to you through this spread? You may choose to ask yourself these questions.

What did I learn and can I now apply it to my life?

How does this information make the situation easier to handle?

What progress have I made since the last time I consulted the cards?

Have any decisions I have made affected my progress?

Have I created any limitations or hesitations in my personal path?

Has this information brought up new questions or areas I need to look at in order to further my growth?

Notes:_____

_____

_____

_____

_____

_____

_____

_____

_____

_____

_____

_____

_____

_____

_____

_____

_____

_____

_____

_____

_____

Daily Progress Sheet

Weekly Progress Sheet

Lesson of the week: Pick one card for the overview or focus of the week you are entering or finishing. Write the name of the card here: _____

Now add that card back into the deck and shuffle the cards before doing a spread of your choice, which will further explain the overview lesson.

Layout and Card Positions

Write your interpretation here and note how these insights may assist your further growth.

_____

_____

_____

_____

_____

_____

_____

_____

_____

_____

_____

_____

_____

_____

_____

_____

_____

_____

_____

_____

_____

_____

Now it might be good to review your earlier progress sheets to see how you are progressing. Are there similar lessons being presented week to week or are you moving quickly through the growth process? If you feel that some of your present lessons are becoming stuck patterns, you might pick one card that expresses the lesson that will assist the energy in flowing again or that will give you a tool with which to meet the challenge being presented.

Daily Progress Sheet

Date: _____   Spread Name: _____

Question or Situation: _____

_____

_____

_____

Layout and Card Positions

How did the cards speak to you through this spread? You may choose to ask yourself these questions.

What did I learn and can I now apply it to my life?

How does this information make the situation easier to handle?

What progress have I made since the last time I consulted the cards?

Have any decisions I have made affected my progress?

Have I created any limitations or hesitations in my personal path?

Has this information brought up new questions or areas I need to look at in order to further my growth?

Notes:_____

_____

_____

_____

_____

_____

_____

_____

_____

_____

_____

_____

_____

_____

_____

_____

_____

_____

_____

_____

　Daily Progress Sheet

Weekly Progress Sheet

Lesson of the week: Pick one card for the overview or focus of the week you are entering or finishing. Write the name of the card here: _____

Now add that card back into the deck and shuffle the cards before doing a spread of your choice, which will further explain the overview lesson.

Layout and Card Positions

Write your interpretation here and note how these insights may assist your further growth.

_____

_____

_____

_____

_____

_____

_____

_____

_____

_____

_____

_____

_____

_____

_____

_____

_____

_____

_____

_____

_____

_____

Now it might be good to review your earlier progress sheets to see how you are progressing. Are there similar lessons being presented week to week or are you moving quickly through the growth process? If you feel that some of your present lessons are becoming stuck patterns, you might pick one card that expresses the lesson that will assist the energy in flowing again or that will give you a tool with which to meet the challenge being presented.

Daily Progress Sheet

Date: _____   Spread Name:_____

Question or Situation: _____

_____

_____

_____

Layout and Card Positions

How did the cards speak to you through this spread? You may choose to ask yourself these questions.

What did I learn and can I now apply it to my life?

How does this information make the situation easier to handle?

What progress have I made since the last time I consulted the cards?

Have any decisions I have made affected my progress?

Have I created any limitations or hesitations in my personal path?

Has this information brought up new questions or areas I need to look at in order to further my growth?

Notes:_____

_____

_____

_____

_____

_____

_____

_____

_____

_____

_____

_____

_____

_____

_____

_____

_____

_____

_____

_____

_____

_____

Weekly Progress Sheet

Lesson of the week: Pick one card for the overview or focus of the week you are entering or finishing. Write the name of the card here: _____

Now add that card back into the deck and shuffle the cards before doing a spread of your choice, which will further explain the overview lesson.

Layout and Card Positions

Write your interpretation here and note how these insights may assist your further growth.

_____

_____

_____

_____

_____

_____

_____

_____

_____

_____

_____

_____

_____

_____

_____

_____

_____

_____

_____

_____

_____

_____

_____

Now it might be good to review your earlier progress sheets to see how you are progressing. Are there similar lessons being presented week to week or are you moving quickly through the growth process? If you feel that some of your present lessons are becoming stuck patterns, you might pick one card that expresses the lesson that will assist the energy in flowing again or that will give you a tool with which to meet the challenge being presented.

Daily Progress Sheet

Date: _____   Spread Name:_____

Question or Situation: _____

_____

_____

_____

Layout and Card Positions

How did the cards speak to you through this spread? You may choose to ask yourself these questions.

What did I learn and can I now apply it to my life?

How does this information make the situation easier to handle?

What progress have I made since the last time I consulted the cards?

Have any decisions I have made affected my progress?

Have I created any limitations or hesitations in my personal path?

Has this information brought up new questions or areas I need to look at in order to further my growth?

Notes:_____

Daily Progress Sheet

Date: _____   Spread Name:_____

Question or Situation: _____

_____

_____

_____

Layout and Card Positions

How did the cards speak to you through this spread? You may choose to ask yourself these questions.

What did I learn and can I now apply it to my life?

How does this information make the situation easier to handle?

What progress have I made since the last time I consulted the cards?

Have any decisions I have made affected my progress?

Have I created any limitations or hesitations in my personal path?

Has this information brought up new questions or areas I need to look at in order to further my growth?

Notes:_____

_____

_____

_____

_____

_____

_____

_____

_____

_____

_____

_____

_____

_____

_____

_____

_____

_____

Daily Progress Sheet

Date: _____ Spread Name:_____

Question or Situation: _____

_____

_____

_____

Layout and Card Positions

How did the cards speak to you through this spread? You may choose to ask yourself these questions.

What did I learn and can I now apply it to my life?

How does this information make the situation easier to handle?

What progress have I made since the last time I consulted the cards?

Have any decisions I have made affected my progress?

Have I created any limitations or hesitations in my personal path?

Has this information brought up new questions or areas I need to look at in order to further my growth?

Notes:_____

_____

_____

_____

_____

_____

_____

_____

_____

_____

_____

_____

_____

_____

_____

_____

_____

_____

_____

Daily Progress Sheet

Date: _____   Spread Name: _____

Question or Situation: _____

_____

_____

_____

Layout and Card Positions

How did the cards speak to you through this spread? You may choose to ask yourself these questions.

What did I learn and can I now apply it to my life?

How does this information make the situation easier to handle?

What progress have I made since the last time I consulted the cards?

Have any decisions I have made affected my progress?

Have I created any limitations or hesitations in my personal path?

Has this information brought up new questions or areas I need to look at in order to further my growth?

Notes:_____

_____

_____

_____

_____

_____

_____

_____

_____

_____

_____

_____

_____

_____

_____

_____

_____

_____

Daily Progress Sheet

Date: _____   Spread Name: _____

Question or Situation: _____

_____

_____

_____

Layout and Card Positions

How did the cards speak to you through this spread? You may choose to ask yourself these questions.

What did I learn and can I now apply it to my life?

How does this information make the situation easier to handle?

What progress have I made since the last time I consulted the cards?

Have any decisions I have made affected my progress?

Have I created any limitations or hesitations in my personal path?

Has this information brought up new questions or areas I need to look at in order to further my growth?

Notes:_____

_____

_____

_____

_____

_____

_____

_____

_____

_____

_____

_____

_____

_____

_____

_____

_____

_____

_____

_____

Daily Progress Sheet

Date: _____   Spread Name:_____

Question or Situation: _____

_____

_____

_____

Layout and Card Positions

How did the cards speak to you through this spread? You may choose to ask yourself these questions.

What did I learn and can I now apply it to my life?

How does this information make the situation easier to handle?

What progress have I made since the last time I consulted the cards?

Have any decisions I have made affected my progress?

Have I created any limitations or hesitations in my personal path?

Has this information brought up new questions or areas I need to look at in order to further my growth?

Notes:_____

_____

_____

_____

_____

_____

_____

_____

_____

_____

_____

_____

_____

_____

_____

_____

_____

_____

_____

_____

_____

Daily Progress Sheet

Date: _____   Spread Name:_____

Question or Situation: _____

_____

_____

_____

Layout and Card Positions

How did the cards speak to you through this spread? You may choose to ask yourself these questions.

What did I learn and can I now apply it to my life?

How does this information make the situation easier to handle?

What progress have I made since the last time I consulted the cards?

Have any decisions I have made affected my progress?

Have I created any limitations or hesitations in my personal path?

Has this information brought up new questions or areas I need to look at in order to further my growth?

Notes:_____

_____

_____

_____

_____

_____

_____

_____

_____

_____

_____

_____

_____

_____

_____

_____

_____

_____

_____

_____

_____

Daily Progress Sheet

Daily Progress Sheet

Date: _____   Spread Name:_____

Question or Situation: _____

_____

_____

_____

Layout and Card Positions

        How did the cards speak to you through this spread? You may choose to
ask yourself these questions.

        What did I learn and can I now apply it to my life?

        How does this information make the situation easier to handle?

        What progress have I made since the last time I consulted the cards?

        Have any decisions I have made affected my progress?

        Have I created any limitations or hesitations in my personal path?

        Has this information brought up new questions or areas I need to look at
            in order to further my growth?

Notes:_____

_____

_____

_____

_____

_____

_____

_____

_____

_____

_____

_____

_____

_____

_____

_____

_____

_____

_____

_____

_____

Daily Progress Sheet

Date: _____   Spread Name:_____

Question or Situation: _____

_____

_____

_____

Layout and Card Positions

How did the cards speak to you through this spread? You may choose to ask yourself these questions.

What did I learn and can I now apply it to my life?

How does this information make the situation easier to handle?

What progress have I made since the last time I consulted the cards?

Have any decisions I have made affected my progress?

Have I created any limitations or hesitations in my personal path?

Has this information brought up new questions or areas I need to look at in order to further my growth?

Notes:_____

_____

_____

_____

_____

_____

_____

_____

_____

_____

_____

_____

_____

_____

_____

_____

_____

_____

_____

_____

_____

_____

Daily Progress Sheet

Date: _____   Spread Name: _____

Question or Situation: _____

_____

_____

_____

Layout and Card Positions

How did the cards speak to you through this spread? You may choose to ask yourself these questions.

What did I learn and can I now apply it to my life?

How does this information make the situation easier to handle?

What progress have I made since the last time I consulted the cards?

Have any decisions I have made affected my progress?

Have I created any limitations or hesitations in my personal path?

Has this information brought up new questions or areas I need to look at in order to further my growth?

Notes:_____

_____

_____

_____

_____

_____

_____

_____

_____

_____

_____

_____

_____

_____

_____

_____

Grow in joy and enjoy your growth!
_____